HANS MEMLING

HANS MEMLING

BY

K. B. McFARLANE

edited by Edgar Wind with
the assistance of G. L. Harriss

CLARENDON PRESS · OXFORD
1971

*Oxford University Press, Ely House, London W.*1

GLASGOW NEW YORK TORONTO MELBOURNE WELLINGTON
CAPE TOWN SALISBURY IBADAN NAIROBI DAR ES SALAAM LUSAKA ADDIS ABABA
BOMBAY CALCUTTA MADRAS KARACHI LAHORE DACCA
KUALA LUMPUR SINGAPORE HONG KONG TOKYO

PRINTED IN GREAT BRITAIN BY ROBERT MACLEHOSE AND CO. LTD,
THE UNIVERSITY PRESS, GLASGOW

Table of Contents

Editor's Note

About the origins of this book on Memling a few particulars gathered from letters and conversation may be of interest.

The crucial discovery that the Donne Triptych had been misdated, from which it follows that the current judgements on Memling's development as an artist are false, was communicated by the author in November 1948 to his friend Professor E. K. Waterhouse and, through him, to Mr. Martin Davies, now director of the National Gallery. Both urged him to publish his observations at once, but with characteristic reticence he remarked that, having approached the subject as a political historian, he could not attempt such a bold foray into art-historical territory without having first undergone a thorough course in *Memling forschung*. It was not until 1957, when the Donne Triptych was transferred from Chatsworth to the National Gallery, that he agreed to read a paper to the Stubbs Society at Oxford, entitled *Hans Memling and an English Patron*. Although the text of that communication was completely written out and seemed to his listeners ready for printing, he again declined to publish his discovery because he still felt uneasy about his art-historical conclusions.

In the winter 1961–2 he wrote for the National Gallery a *Memorandum on the Date of the Donne Triptych*, with the understanding that the compiler of the National Gallery Catalogue (Mr. Davies) should feel free to use these observations as he saw fit. About the same time, or a little earlier, the Department of the History of Art in Oxford invited McFarlane to give eight lectures on Memling. These were delivered in the Trinity term 1962 and proved so convincing, even to the lecturer himself, that he decided he was ready to produce a book: but he died in the course of its preparation.

The present edition is only a shadow of the *Memling* that McFarlane would have published. Part I presents the arguments of the Stubbs paper, revised and expanded with the help of rough notes jotted down by the author for that purpose. Parts II and III are taken from the papers he had prepared for his University lectures, again revised in the light of later notes. For the sake of completeness the *Memorandum* written for the National Gallery has been added in an Appendix, again in a form brought up to date. The editorial adjustments made necessary by the revisions were less difficult than had been expected: for in every instance in which a choice had to be made between several versions, the latest in time seemed the most circumspect and also the most felicitous.

A much more difficult problem was posed by the many hints contained in the rough notes for further clarification and research, which the author was not given the chance to carry out but of which he had spoken in private, often in great detail. Here, after consultation with Mr. McFarlane's friends, pupils and colleagues, it was decided to take a calculated risk by assuming that his intentions would be better served by scrupulously pursuing his arguments to their conclusion than by publishing them incomplete.

The original plan was to place any additions to the author's own words in square brackets, but since these ungainly signals would have interrupted his text and made the reading of it unduly cumbersome, it seemed more reasonable to meet the problem by depositing all the original papers in the McFarlane Library at Magdalen College, where they would be open to consultation. Only in one case – the long Note added to Part II – did the editor feel the need to distinguish his work from that of the author: because no hint could be found either in Mr. McFarlane's papers, or remembered from his conversation, that he had planned to pursue that particular trail. It seemed nevertheless right to do so because the bold guess about the Danzig *Last Judgement*, the only instance in which the author surrendered to intuition ('an admission of failure', as he called it), will appear less stark if it is combined with subsidiary evidence, apparently unsuspected by him at the time. All in all, it can be said that although the workmanship of this book is 'by several hands', it is the work of one man.

Those who heard McFarlane's lectures on Memling in 1962 may notice that we have used only those portions of them that embody his own discoveries. Stylistic analyses, descriptive passages and discussions of schoolworks and of dubious attributions have been retained only in so far as they form part of the central argument. The few points on which he was in agreement with the officially accepted view (for example, in the distinction between various backgrounds in Memling's portraits, or between the floor patterns that he favoured) are not repeated here in any detail because these touches of conventional art history, which may be gathered equally well (perhaps even better) from the more conventional books on Memling, might obfuscate the original discoveries, from which a new view of Memling emerges. The sequence of the plates, apart from illustrating the argument, is meant to show the range and quality of this rediscovered master.

The editor's thanks are due to the executrix of Mr. McFarlane's will, Dr. Helena Wright, for her personal kindness and support; to Mr. K. J. Leyser for invaluable guidance and much encouragement; to Mr. J. P. Cooper and Dr. J. R. L. Highfield for several constructive observations; to Dr. M. G. A. Vale, who kindly assisted the editor with his advice and gave initial help with the references, though he must not be held responsible for their final form or for any conclusions drawn from them; to Professor Austin Gill and Mr. Colin Hardie for their meticulous scrutiny of the text, which they were good enough to read in proof-stage; to Dr. T. S. R. Boase for the interest he took in a variety of tentative plans for the book; to Dr. C. V. H. Sutherland and Dr. C. M. Kraay for help on a numismatic problem; and quite particularly to Dr. G. L. Harriss for the precision, patience and generous energy that he spent on refining and completing the historical documentation. While the sources of the photographs are listed below, special thanks for exceptional services are due to the National Museum in Warsaw in connexion with the Danzig *Last Judgement*; to the Institut Royal du Patrimoine Artistique in Brussels for copies from their magnificent photographic archives (A.C.L.); and to the photographic department at the National Gallery in London for their unfailing response to difficult requests in connexion with the Donne Altarpiece. The editor also wishes to thank the officers of the Clarendon Press for the elegant design and scrupulous production of the book.

E. W.

Oxford
September 1970

List of Illustrations

Sources of Photographs

Alinari, Florence (figs. 70, 72–76, 135–136, 140); Anderson, Rome (figs. 149–150); Archives Photographiques, Paris (fig. 60); Ashmolean Museum, Oxford (fig. 142b); Bayerische Staatsgemäldesammlungen, Munich (figs. 71, 77–81); Paul Bijtebier, Brussels (figs. 18, 30–31, 88–89, 91); Boymans-van Beuningen Museum, Rotterdam (fig. 138); J. E. Bulloz, Paris (figs. 17, 39, 44, 49, 95, 99, 110, 141); Wilhelm Castelli, Lübeck (figs. 111–131); Institut Royal du Patrimoine Artistique, A. C. L., Brussels (figs. 11, 13–16, 19–27, 32–36, 59, 82–87, 90, 94, 98, 100–104, 106–108, 139, 148, 151–152); Kunsthistorisches Museum, Vienna (fig. 69); Mauritshuis, The Hague (fig. 147); Metropolitan Museum of Art, New York (figs. 133–134, 137); Musée de l'Hôtel-Dieu, Beaune (fig. 50); Musée Royal des Beaux-Arts, Brussels (figs. 92–93); National Gallery, London (figs. 1–10, 37, 143, 153); National Gallery of Art, Washington (fig. 132); National Gallery of Canada, Ottawa (fig. 38); National Museum, Warsaw (figs. 40–43, 45–48, 51–58, 61, 65–68); Staatliche Museen, Berlin-Dahlem: Photo Walter Steinkopf (figs. 28, 146); Collection Baron H. H. Thyssen-Bornemisza, Lugano (figs. 144–145); Wallace Collection, London (fig. 109).

PART I

Hans Memling and an English Patron

THE Chatsworth altarpiece (figs. 1-10), acquired by the National Gallery from the Duke of Devonshire in 1957, is generally held to be the earliest painting by Hans Memling to which it is possible to assign a more or less certain date.[1] A good deal too much, it may be thought, has been made to depend upon this far from well-tested assumption. It has helped, for example, to fix the year of Memling's birth.[2] It has also given rise to the theory that the artist may have paid an otherwise unrecorded visit to England soon after establishing himself at Bruges in 1465.[3] Most important of all, it has been held to settle the character of his artistic development. The triptych, so runs the argument, betrays little or no evidence of immaturity in comparison with Memling's later work. Since it was certainly executed before 1469 and very probably as early as 1466,[4] it must therefore follow that Memling's genius, after ripening fully in his early manhood, henceforward possessed no capacity to evolve. Both his style and the quality of his execution are shown to have remained static.[5] Such deductions might indeed be inevitable were the premise from which they start established beyond question. Yet it is not difficult to show that there is no real foundation for the accepted date.

It is based on the belief that the 'donor' who kneels in the foreground of the central panel (fig. 3) and who was identified more than a century ago as Sir John Donne of Kidwelly,[6] was slain at the battle of Edgecote on 26

[1] Max J. Friedländer, *Die altniederländische Malerei* VI (1928), pp. 13, 117 no. 10; following the more detailed demonstration of G. Hulin de Loo in *Festschrift für Max J. Friedländer* (1927), pp. 103-8. Of earlier literature see W. H. J. Weale, 'Triptych by Hans Memling at Chiswick', *Notes and Queries* VI (1864), pp. 451 f.; L. Kaemmerer, *Memling* (1899), p. 28; Weale, *Hans Memlinc* (1901), pp. 13-17; K. Voll, *Memling* (1909), pp. xiv-xvi; Friedländer, *Von Eyck bis Bruegel* (1916), pp. 56, 58.

[2] Friedländer, *ibid.*, p. 56; also *Die altniederländische Malerei* VI, p. 14.

[3] Hulin de Loo, *op. cit.*, p. 104.

[4] *ibid.*

[5] Friedländer, *Die altniederländische Malerei* VI, p. 14; 'Alles kehrt wieder in später entstandenen Gemälden ... weil ... der Meister schon um 1468 die ihn befriedigende Lösung ... gefunden hatte'; also Hulin de Loo, *op. cit.*, pp. 103 f.

[6] By J. Gough Nichols in *The Gentleman's Magazine* II (1840), pp. 489 ff. As early as 1838, G. F. Waagen (*Works of Art and Artists in England* I, p. 268) had come across the Donne Altarpiece at Chiswick, hanging so high that he could barely see it, but he guessed nevertheless that it must be a Memling. The donor's name he did not

July 1469.[7] There is no good reason for doubting the identification, which is derived from heraldic evidence on the painting itself. On the capital of the column next to the Virgin's canopy immediately behind the male donor, and again in the window beside St. John the Evangelist on the right wing of the triptych, appears a shield with these arms: Azure, a wolf rampant argent (figs. 6, 153). On the corresponding capital behind the female donor will be found the same arms impaling Argent, a maunch sable (fig. 7). The latter is the well-known coat of the family of Hastings,[8] whose head in 1529 was created Earl of Huntingdon. The former, though much less familiar, is ascribed by Glover and other later heralds to the Donnes of Kidwelly.[9] Finally there is good contemporary evidence for the fact that Elizabeth, daughter of Sir Leonard Hastings (who died in October 1455[10]), was the wife of Sir John Donne.[11] It is difficult to avoid the conclusion that she and her husband are the donors depicted in the Memling altarpiece. But the evidence for Sir John's death at Edgecote is far more disputable.

It is derived in fact from a single contemporary source, namely a list of casualties given by John Warkworth, Master of Peterhouse 1473–1500, in his short continuation to Caxton's *Chronicles of England*.[12] It is noteworthy that a similar list preserved in the Itinerary of William of Worcester gives the Christian name of the Donne of Kidwelly who was killed as Henry, John's older brother.[13] It may well be doubted whether any *John* Donne fell at Edgecote. That the husband of Elizabeth Hastings did not is conclusively proved by her brother William's will, drawn up on 27 June 1481 and proved two years later after his execution.[14] It is only

know. In later editions of Waagen's work the painting is no longer listed, either as at Chatsworth or at Chiswick, where it actually remained until December 1892 (see Martin Davies, *National Gallery Catalogue: Early Netherlandish School*, 1968, p. 127).

[7] On the crucial importance of this date for the current chronology of Memling's works, see the literature quoted above, note 1.

[8] According to N. Harris Nicolas (*The Controversy between Sir Richard Scrope and Sir Robert Grosvenor in the Court of Chivalry, A.D. 1385–1390* II, 1832, p. 285, with documentary note), these arms were borne by Sir Ralph Hastings in Edward III's reign.

[9] J. W. Papworth and A. W. Morant, *Alphabetical Dictionary of Coats of Arms* (1874), p. 98.

[10] *Calendar of Fine Rolls, 1452–61*, p. 135: writ of *diem clausit extremum*, dated 25 October 1455.

[11] The will of William lord Hastings, 27 June 1481 (Prerogative Court of Canterbury, 10 Logge), refers to 'my sister Dame Elizabeth Donne' and 'my brother Sir John Donne'; see below, page 3. The name, in Welsh Dwn, is variously spelt Don, Doun, Donne, etc. I have adopted the spelling Donne wherever possible.

[12] *A Chronicle of the First Thirteen Years of the Reign of King Edward IV*, ed. J. O. Halliwell (Camden Society 1839), pp. 6 f.

[13] William Worcestre, *Itineraries*, ed. John H. Harvey (1969), pp. 340 f. Both lists also contain the name of a cousin, Henry Donne of Picton. On Henry Donne of Kidwelly see more specifically *ibid.*, pp. 338 ff.

[14] See above, note 11. A somewhat inaccurate transcript of the will was printed by N. Harris Nicolas, *Testamenta vetusta* I (1826), pp. 368–75.

necessary to quote two bequests from this long and interesting document: 'Also I will that mine executors give to my sister Dame Elizabeth Donne c[= 100] marks. . . . Also where I have the ward and marriage of Edward Trussell, I will that it be sold and the money employed to the performing of this my will and for the weal of my soul; and if my brother Sir John Donne will buy the said ward, I will that he be preferred therein before any other by xl *li*.' Twelve years, therefore, after Edgecote Sir John was still alive. His own will and that of his wife make it certain that he died in his bed in late January or early February 1503.[15] Strange to say, none of the historians of Memling who have accepted the date 1469 as their *terminus ante quem* seems to have inquired when and where the man whom they knew as Sir John Donne had received his knighthood: it was on the field of Tewkesbury on 4 May 1471,[16] two years after the battle of Edgecote, at which they supposed that he had been slain.

A certain unease is plainly detectable in the attempts to work out more exactly in what year before 1469 Memling's altarpiece would have been painted. It was known, for example, that in addition to the young daughter kneeling behind Lady Donne in the central panel, Donne's wife had borne him two sons. Since, if they had already existed, they could not have been omitted from such a devotional family group,[17] that made it certain that Memling executed his commission *not later than 1468*; indeed, 1468 was cutting it very fine, but some historians of Memling preferred it because the marriage of Margaret of York to Charles of Burgundy in that year

[15] John Donne's will (Prerogative Court of Canterbury, 10 Blamyr) is dated 23 January 1502(3); his wife's (P. C. C. 32 Adeane) is 29 November 1507. Sir John was certainly dead by 13 February 1502(3), when his will was proved (Lambeth), and George Talbot earl of Shrewsbury wrote to Sir Reynold Bray 'to be good master unto my wife's aunt Dame Elizabeth Donne in such matters as she will labour unto you' (Westminster Abbey Muniments 16057). The fact that Sir John left both lands and goods to his widow suggests that his eldest son, Edward, was not yet of age in 1502(3). Lady Donne's will appointed Edward her sole executor and residuary legatee; and this will was proved Lambeth 15 February 1507(8). The absence of an *inquisitio post mortem* on Sir John Donne suggests that he had enfeoffed all his English freeholds to uses before his death.

[16] See W. A. Shaw, *The Knights of England* II (1906), p. 14.

[17] The rule, first clearly recognized in 1902 by A. Warburg (*Gesammelte Schriften*, 1932, p. 197 note 7), then freshly observed by Hulin de Loo (*Festschrift Friedländer*, pp. 103 f.) and raised by E. Panofsky to an infrangible law (*Early Netherlandish Painting*, 1953, p. 500: 'The omission even of babes in arms from a donation of this kind would have amounted to a *diminutio capitis* . . . .'), is not so much an historical generalization, in which case one would have to allow for exceptions, as a liturgical imperative comparable in its rigidity to the rules of heraldry or of royal etiquette. Since the purpose of these devotional portrait-groups was to invoke divine protection through the intercession of saints, it would be indeed inconceivable to exclude any of the donor's children from the invocation. The faceless heads that conclude the large group of daughters in the Moreel altarpiece (figs. 85, 91) show that if they could not all be portrayed they were at least all counted. Needless to say, the rule applies to devotional group-portraits only, not to any secular groups; nor does it extend to half-lengths or bust-portraits of individuals in prayer, such as figs. 92 f., 133 f., 143 f., 147, 150, 152.

offered a ready explanation of the Donnes' being at Bruges.[18] The fact that both husband and wife were shown wearing the Yorkist livery-collar, with Edward IV's personal badge, the lion of March, as a pendant (figs. 3, 4),[19] reinforced the belief that they were in Margaret's wedding-party; and there is direct evidence to support that view.[20] On the other hand Hulin de Loo, thinking 1468 too close a fit for two further children, suggested that Memling might have painted the picture in England in 1466, having supposedly accompanied the Burgundian envoys who that year came to seek Margaret's hand.[21] Although there is no evidence of Memling's participation in that voyage, it must be confessed that, on the given assumptions, 1466 would be the preferable date, especially when it is discovered that in addition to the two sons a second daughter has to be found a birthday after the picture was painted, the Donnes having had four children who survived infancy, not three.[22]

It was of course recognised that Memling could not have received the commission before he was firmly established in Bruges, where he settled in 1465. This seemed as certain a *terminus post quem* as 1469 was a *terminus ante*. If opinions wavered between 1466 and 1468, it was only because of the question of how many children Sir John could have produced in the short interval between the completion of the painting and his supposed death. Had some of the dates concerning the lives of these children been known, the doubt would have changed into consternation.

Another source of embarrassment was the close affinity between the Donne altarpiece and the *Mystic Marriage of St. Catherine* in the hospital at Bruges (fig. 35), which is dated 1479 on the frame.[23] There is considerable

[18] Weale, *Hans Memlinc*, p. 17; Friedländer, *Von Eyck bis Bruegel*, p. 56; *Die altniederländische Malerei* VI, p. 13.

[19] Since portraits with Yorkist livery collars are rare, it may be worth noting that in Melbury Sampford Church, Dorset, the effigy of William Brouning senior wears the collar of suns and roses with the lion of March as pendant (*Royal Commission on Historical Monuments, West Dorset*, 1952, p. 162, pl. 23). The man had been Richard duke of York's receiver for Somerset and Dorset since at least 1436-7, and continued there as surveyor for the rest of his life (K. B. McFarlane, *The Wars of the Roses*, Raleigh Lecture, British Academy, 1964, pp. 90 f. note 2). His effigy suggests that his retention in office by Henry VI (*Cal. Pat. Rolls, 1452-61*, p. 592) is insufficient ground for describing him as 'obviously a good Lancastrian' (J. C. Wedgwood in *History of Parliament 1439-1509: Biographies*, 1936, p. 125).

[20] *Mémoires d'Olivier de la Marche*, ed. H. Beaune and J. d'Arbaumont, III (1885), p. 111. Although Donne is mentioned alone, it is not unreasonable to suppose that both he and his wife were in attendance.

[21] *Festschrift Friedländer*, p. 104.

[22] See below, pages 8 f. and 53 ff.

[23] Weale, *Hans Memlinc*, pp. 40, 97; P. Coremans, R. Sneyers and J. Thissen, 'Memlinc's Mystiek Hulwelijk van de H. Katharina, Onderzoek en Behandeling', *Bulletin de l'Institut Royal du Patrimoine Artistique* II (1959), pp. 83-96. The fact that the inscription on the frame was retraced in the nineteenth century (*ibid.*, pp. 85 f., 95) does not mean that it is untrustworthy. Unless there are cogent reasons to the contrary, it may be assumed that it repeats an older inscription, particularly as regards the date 1479.

difference in size, the Chatsworth panel being 2 ft. 4 ins. high as against the 5 ft. 8 ins. of the *Mystic Marriage*; and the connoisseurship of Friedländer when brought to bear on the smaller picture had noticed that its 'early style . . . is betrayed mainly by the thin, anaemic and dry treatment.'[24] Nevertheless there are striking similarities: not only are the four saints of the one also found in the other, but they have the same faces and in the case of the two St. Johns almost the same poses. When a picture painted in 1466 differs so little in conception and execution from another produced thirteen years later, is it surprising that Hans Memling should be thought prematurely set in his ways? 'At the point where the documentation of the artist begins, he has chosen his way definitely and is in full possession of his talent.' So Hulin pronounces the inevitable judgement.[25] But nevertheless he is puzzled: 'Memling remained stationary' in the sense that he reached the limits of his capacity straight away. As Friedländer put it in 1939 at the time of the great Memling exhibition at Bruges, the historian does not find 'a real field of activity' in Memling: 'The development of this master appears like a continuous, gentle sliding with no sudden turnings.'[26] Even the clairvoyant connoisseur, it seems, was here in need of some external assistance, finding himself sliding uncomfortably down the years, unable to find anything of which to catch hold. One thing that never occurred to him was that the Donne triptych had all the time been misdated.

It remains to be seen whether a collection of the known facts about John Donne's career makes it possible to establish the real date of the Chatsworth altarpiece with a fair degree of probability.

The Donnes of Kidwelly were, it seems, members of one of those numerous families of small Welsh gentry who managed to do well out of the second half of the Hundred Years War.[27] Kidwelly belonged to the Dukes of Lancaster, and Donnes are found in the service of John of Gaunt.[28]

---

[24] *Von Eyck bis Bruegel*, p. 59: 'Memling . . . vergleichsweise selbständig . . . schon im Devonshire=Triptychon, das sich als Frühwerk hauptsächlich durch *dünne, blutlose und trockene Behandlung* verrät' (italics ours).

[25] *Festschrift Friedländer*, loc. cit. The only dissenting voice among Memling scholars was that of Franz Bock, *Memling-Studien* (1900), pp. 177-81, who found the early date given to the Chatsworth triptych so improbable that he began to doubt whether the donor had been correctly identified as Sir John Donne, whose death at Edgecote in 1469 he did not question.

[26] 'The Memling Exhibition at Bruges,' *The Burlington Magazine* LXXV (1939), pp. 123 f.

[27] The ap Williams (afterwards Herberts, earls of Pembroke) and their kinsmen the Vaughans are perhaps the best-known examples of this class. They were both connexions of the Donnes. For a general summary of rewards obtained by Welshmen who had fought in France, see A. D. Carr, 'Welshmen and the Hundred Years' War', *The Welsh History Review* IV (1968), pp. 44 ff.

[28] *John of Gaunt's Register, 1379-83*, ed. E. C. Lodge

A Henry Donne was a supporter of Owen Glendower when the latter rose in rebellion against Henry IV.[29] This Donne was evidently a person of some local importance. Unlike his leader he survived the rebellion and obtained a royal pardon in 1413.[30] At this date he must have been well on in years, since according to the Welsh genealogists, whose doubtful authority is here reinforced by the records, he was by his son Meredith the grandfather of Griffith Donne;[31] and Griffith was already making a name for himself as a soldier in the French wars before the death of Henry V.[32] Enough is known about him and his family to make it likely that the birth of his third and youngest son, John, took place about 1430, though not later. In Memling's painting he looks a none too young fifty, to judge by the thinning hair and the wrinkled forehead, eyes and neck (fig. 3).

Like his two elder brothers, John Donne was born in France;[33] and since his father served there in the retinue of Richard duke of York,[34] there is a

and R. Somerville, I (Camden Society 1937), no. 621; II, no. 827.

[29] T. W. Newton Dunn, *Genealogies of the Dwnns of South Wales* (1953), p. 8, referring to an Assize roll of Kidwelly for 1411. See also *Cartularium S. Johannis Bapt. de Caermarthen*, ed. T[homas] P[hillipps], (1865), pp. 50 f., nos. 125 f.; *Welsh Records in Paris*, ed. T. Matthews (1910), pp. 105 f.; *Original Letters illustrative of English History*, ed. Henry Ellis, I (1827), pp. 13 ff.; *Royal and Historical Letters during the Reign of Henry IV*, ed. F. C. Hingeston, I (Rolls series 1860), pp. 138–40, 160–2; J. E. Lloyd, *Owen Glendower* (1931), pp. 40 f.

[30] *Cal. Pat. Rolls, 1413–16*, pp. 29, 44. He may have been the Henry Donne who was one of the provosts of Pembroke, 12 December 1419 (*Descriptive Catalogue of Ancient Deeds* III, 1900, no. D.535).

[31] See Lewys Dwnn, *Heraldic Visitations of Wales*, ed. S. R. Meyrick, I (1846), p. 222; supported by the Assize roll of 1411 (above, note 29), which shows that Henry Donne of Kidwelly had a son named Meredith; and further by the pardon of 30 May 1413, which included Griffith ap Meredith ap Henry (*Cal. Pat. Rolls, 1413–16*, p. 29).

[32] *Cal. Pat. Rolls, 1422–9*, p. 397. Griffith Donne's petition to be allowed to buy land in England and to enjoy all the liberties of the king's English subjects despite the fact that both his parents were Welsh was granted in the parliament of May 1421 (*Rotuli Parliamentorum* IV, pp. 130 f.). That same month he received letters of protection going to France in the retinue of Sir Walter Hungerford (*Reports of the Deputy Keeper of the Public Records* XLIV, 1883, p. 622). He was lieutenant of Cherbourg in 1424 (H. de Frondeville, *La Vicomté d'Orbec pendant l'occupation anglaise 1417–49*, Lisieux 1936, p. 242 note 329).

[33] Worcester, *Itineraries*, pp. 338 ff.: 'Gryffyth Don habuit 3 filios in Francia: Robertus Don non maritavit; Henricus Don in Francia maritavit filiam Sir Roger Vaghan chivaler et mortuus apud Banberyfelde; tercius filius minor Johannes Don, qui maritavit filiam [*recte* sororem] domini de Hastyngys Chambyrleyn camerarii regis.' If Elizabeth Hastings were some twenty years younger than her famous brother, Worcester could surely be excused for having mistaken her for his daughter. That John Donne was born in France is confirmed by his letters of naturalization in England (*Cal. Pat. Rolls, 1467–77*, p. 86): 'John Donne of Calais, born in Picardy'.

[34] He had joined York's retinue in 1436 (*Reports of the Deputy Keeper of the Public Records* XLVIII, 1887, p. 310) and was captain of Carentan in 1437, of Tancarville in 1438, of Neufchâtel in 1441, of Lisieux in 1441 and 1442, and of Gaillan at a later date (Frondeville, *La Vicomté d'Orbec*, p. 242 note 329). His most famous military exploit was the capture of Raoul sire de Gaucourt during the siege of Harfleur, whose garrison then surrendered, in 1440 (see Jehan de Waurin, *Recueil des croniques et anchiennes istories de la Grant Bretaigne* IV, *1431–47*, ed. W. and E. L. C. P. Hardy, 1884, p. 278; also Worcester, *Itineraries*, p. 341). At the recommendation of the Duke of York (Frondeville, p. 244) he received, in recognition of his services, the lordship of Auqueville and the fiefs of Ortier and Fervaques (see texts in Frondeville, pp. 242–7, nos. 329, 331, 333; also Carr, 'Welshmen and the Hundred Years' War', p. 46). Although reported by Newton Dunn as still active in the defence of Normandy as late as 1449 (*The Genealogies of the Dwnns*, p. 12, no. 39), he was in fact dead by 1448, when his eldest son Robert, engaged in a law-suit against Durant de Thieuville, is cited as 'Robert Don, écuyer, seigneur de Fervaques, fils aîné et principal héritier de Griffith Don'

strong presumption that he started his career in the same army before the fall of Normandy in 1450, and then continued to serve the duke in Ireland and England: for he was handsomely rewarded after the accession of Edward IV 'for his good service to the king's father Richard, late duke of York, in England, France and Ireland'.[35] He remained a loyal and increasingly trusted follower of the house of York thereafter.[36] In or before 1465, in any case after February 1462, he married Elizabeth Hastings,[37] whose brother was already prominent in Edward IV's favour. Henceforward his fortunes were closely bound up with those of Hastings, though he escaped disaster when his brother-in-law was executed by Richard III.

Elizabeth Hastings was the youngest daughter and possibly the youngest child of the large family of Sir Leonard Hastings and Alice Camoys (through whom she was descended from the Mortimer earls of March). Her marriage took place some ten or more years later than that of her next oldest sister[38] and is consistent with her birth as late as 1450. It is likely

(Frondeville, p. 242 note 329).

[35] *Cal. Pat. Rolls, 1461–7*, p. 111 (24 February 1462), restated more explicitly in *Cal. Pat. Rolls, 1467–77*, p. 59, where Donne's service 'to the king's father Richard, late duke of York, in England, France and Ireland' is distinguished from his service 'to the king in battle against Henry VI and Jasper, earl of Pembroke, and James, earl of Wiltshire, and other rebels.' The formula used in the second part is exactly the same as in the well-known document rewarding William Hastings in 1461: 'tam contra magnum adversarium nostrum Henricum sextum . . . quam contra Jasperem Pembrochie et Jacobum Wiltes' nuper Comites aliosque rebelles' (*The Complete Peerage* VI, 1926, p. 371 note a). It follows that Donne participated, with Hastings and Sir William Herbert, in the campaign of Mortimer's Cross in February 1461. The reference to Ireland in the first citation may well indicate that he had been with the Duke of York at Ludford in October 1459 and subsequently joined him in Ireland (compare similar citations for James Manthorp, Thomas Colt, Robert Fitz Eustace and Robert Bernewall in *Cal. Pat. Rolls, 1461–7*, pp. 83, 85, 117, 178, 188). On the Duke's large contingent of Welsh retainers see J. Gairdner in *Dictionary of National Biography*, s.v. 'Richard, duke of York'. As for Donne's service to the Duke in France, this must have been performed prior to 1447 because in that year the Duke of York ceased to be the King's lieutenant in France and Normandy and (except for the short period from November 1454 to March 1455 when he was nominally captain of Calais) never held any command in France thereafter. (On the failure of the Duke's bid for Calais see G. L. Harriss, 'The Struggle for Calais: an aspect of the

rivalry between Lancaster and York', *The English Historical Review* LXXV, 1960, pp. 30–53). For a possible parallel to the French part of Donne's citation see *Cal. Pat. Rolls, 1461–7*, p. 83, grant to Nicholas Pemberton, which refers unmistakably back to 1440–50 since Normandy is explicitly mentioned. The inference that if Donne served the Duke of York in France before 1447 he cannot have been born later than 1430 is supported by the fact that Membling's portrait, which *must* have been painted before 1483 because of the livery collar worn by John Donne, shows him as a none too young fifty (fig. 3).

[36] As early as 12 August 1461 (*Cal. Pat. Rolls, 1461–7*, p. 38) he had been appointed to a commission 'to enquire into all treasons, insurrections and rebellions in South Wales'; and he received rewards on 9 September 1461 (*ibid.*, p. 40), modest compared to those that were to follow on 24 February 1462 (*ibid.*, p. 111), when he had become an usher of the chamber in the King's household.

[37] 'Elizabeth his wife' is mentioned for the first time together with John Donne, 'esquire of the body', in the regranting of royal favours on 11 March 1465 (*Cal. Pat. Rolls, 1461–7*, p. 430), previously granted on 24 February 1462 without mention of wife (*ibid.*, p. 111). Since the date of the new patent was determined by the act of resumption of royal grants passed by Parliament in the session of January – March 1465, it offers no immediate evidence for the date of Donne's marriage, except as a *terminus ante quem*. The inclusion of his wife in the new grant would, of course, be particularly appropriate if there were a marked disparity of age, so that she could expect to outlive him while his heir was still a minor.

[38] For the marriage covenant of her sister Joan, dated 24 May 1453, see *Historical Manuscripts Commission, Rawdon*

therefore that she was some twenty years her husband's junior (even though she survived him by only about five years). The younger son of a Welsh military adventurer had to wait before he was in a position to marry. That came for Donne after he had been rewarded for his share in the usurpation of 1461. That in the triptych his wife could be thirty or even less is, I think, conceivable (fig. 4), but the putative ages of the donors (the dates of their births being unknown) are not going to settle the question of the picture's date. We may note, however, that they do not contradict or render noticeably unlikely the placing of that date about 1480.

What of the births of their children? If the girl in the triptych survived, then she was Anne, afterwards the first wife of Sir William Rede of Boarstall. Her husband was born in 1467.[39] Since his marriage to Anne Donne was arranged by their families we may suspect that his bride was rather younger than he (as was usual), but cannot be sure.[40] Her birth in the same year as her husband's is possible, but 1470–1 is the more likely date and it may well have been later. A date before 1467 is most improbable. Hence, if the picture were dated 1468, she would have been, at best, only one year old, and in 1466 it is virtually certain that she was not yet born. But quite apart from Anne Donne's marriage, the probability that the Donnes themselves were married about 1465 makes it unlikely that either in 1466 or in 1468 they had a child of the age shown in the painting.

That Anne was the eldest of the Donne's children, in so far as they survived infancy, can be established without much difficulty. The son and heir, Sir Edward, knighted in 1513, was still alive on Christmas Eve 1551, and died about the beginning of 1552.[41] He does not seem to have been of

Hastings MSS I (1928), pp. 300 f., no. 1277. The next oldest sister, Anne, was married in 1448 (*ibid.*, no. 1276).

[39] He was twenty-two years old in 1489, when he succeeded to the lands of his grandfather Sir Edmund Rede (*The Boarstall Cartulary*, ed. H. E. Salter, 1930, pp. 286–95; *Calendar of Inquisitions post mortem, Henry VII*, I, nos. 465–7), and thirty years old in 1498 (*ibid.*, nos. 237 f.). He settled Boarstall in 1511, perhaps soon after his second marriage, and must have died in or before 1527, when Boarstall passed to his son Leonard (*Victoria County History, Buckinghamshire* IV, 1927, p. 12), on whom see next note.

[40] Anne Donne died almost certainly before her mother made her will, 29 November 1507 (on which see above, note 15), since this refers to Anne's children but not to her. She had two daughters, Elizabeth and Mary, and a son, Leonard, who was probably of age by 1521 when

he was one of eight feoffees who were to benefit from a licence to alienate part of the manor of Gynge (*Letters and Papers, Foreign and Domestic, of the Reign of Henry VIII*, ed. J. S. Brewer, III, i, 1867, no. 1262). He was presumably named after his mother's maternal grandfather Sir Leonard Hastings. His step-mother (whose name, Anne, has caused some confusion with the first Lady Rede) was a niece of Archbishop Warham and apparently an important member of the Princess Mary's household. This is shown by her correspondence, which reveals also severe altercations with her step-son over her jointure (*Letters and Papers, Henry VIII*, IV, i, p. 77; IV, ii, nos. 2577, 2854, 3029, 3226, 3367, 3589, 4152).

[41] His will (Prerogative Court of Canterbury, F. 1 Powell) is dated 20 December 5 Edward VI [= 1551], with a codicil of 24 December. In 1527 he was Sheriff of Buckinghamshire and frequently served on Com-

age at his father's death in 1503, which puts his birth in or after 1482. His brother Sir Griffith, the jousting companion of the future Henry VIII, was obviously his junior, so there is no difficulty about him.[42] That leaves the Donnes' only other known child Margaret. She was married by her father to his ward Edward Trussell and her first child was born in 1496, when her husband was eighteen.[43] She is unlikely to have been born after 1481, but since marriages were then frequently if not usually consummated when the bride was fourteen, there is no reason to place her birth much earlier.[44] If we are right in assigning her sister Anne's birth to the years 1467–71, hers should belong to the years 1478–81 (1478 being the birthdate of her husband). It follows that as late as 1479–80 the Donnes may have been painted in the company of a single child.

Lastly, when could Donne and his family have sat to Memling? The answer is, at almost any time. Apart from an embassy to the French court in February and March 1477[45] he could easily have been at Bruges in any year between 1470 (if not before) and Edward IV's death. As an esquire of the king's body[46] it is very likely that he accompanied Edward on his flight from England to the Low Countries in 1470–1; his brother-in-law Hastings certainly did. But these months of exile and diplomatic and military preparation at Bruges were not exactly the most suitable in which to commission and pay for a triptych. Money was short and was needed for the reconquest of England. But from 1471 onwards Hastings was the king's lieutenant of Calais and within a short time there is evidence that Donne was occupying responsible office there under his brother-in-law. On 18 June 1472[47] he was one of those appointed to treat with the Burgundian envoys about delimiting the frontiers of the English Pale towards Picardy. He was present in 1475 when Edward IV met Charles and Margaret of Burgundy,[48] and during the military operations of that summer

missions of the Peace (*Letters and Papers, Henry VIII*, IV, ii, nos. 3581, 6460, 6751). His parents' wills (see above, note 15) permit some inference on the date of his birth (cp. also below, page 53), after January 1482 but not later than November 1486.

[42] See below, page 54, for details concerning Sir Griffith Donne.

[43] On Edward Trussel and his two children Elizabeth and John, aged three and one when their father died under age in the spring of 1499, see *Calendar of Inquisitions post mortem, Henry VII*, II, nos. 326, 407; III, no. 234; also I, no. 726, for the calculable date of Edward Trussell's birth (aged fourteen in 1492).

[44] It should be noted, however, that on 27 June 1481, when William Hastings drew up his will, he took account of Donne's possible interest in buying the wardship of Edward Trussell (see above, page 3). This would seem to imply that Margaret Donne was born before 27 June 1481.

[45] C. L. Scofield, *The Life and Reign of Edward IV*, II (1923), pp. 177–83.

[46] *Cal. Pat. Rolls, 1461–7*, p. 430; *1467–77*, p. 175; also British Museum Harleian MS 642, fol. 178ᵛ; cf. A. R. Myers, *The Household of Edward IV* (1959), p. 199.

[47] T. Rymer, *Foedera* XI (1710), p. 759.

[48] On 12 May 1475 (*Cal. Pat. Rolls 1467–77*, p. 517) Donne is named among the feoffees of William lord Hastings

he stayed behind in Calais to provide a link between the royal army advancing into France and the English council across the Channel. In May 1477 he was sent to Ghent[49] to negotiate with the Imperial ambassadors in connexion with the marriage of Edward's niece, Mary of Burgundy, to Maximilian of Habsburg. In the summer of 1483 he is mentioned as one of the English commanders in Calais,[50] and later under Henry VII (before 1497) he was himself its lieutenant.[51] After his death his widow continued to occupy a house there.[52] Not much more than 60 miles from Bruges, the Donnes at Calais were within easy reach of Memling's workshop for most of the artist's active life.

We must then free ourselves of the notion that it would require a grand official occasion, such as the marriage of Margaret of York to Charles of Burgundy, to account for the presence of Sir John Donne in Bruges. In that city the Hospital of Saint John, being associated with Donne's name-saints, John the Baptist and John the Evangelist, was probably his favourite place of worship, and the fact that he dedicated his own altarpiece not only to the two St. Johns, but also to St. Catherine and St. Barbara who appear with them on the High Altar at Bruges (fig. 35), suggests that he was anxious to retain for his private worship the group of saints that he had come to cherish.[53] If the triptych he ordered bears a close resemblance to the one completed for Bruges in 1479, it is reasonable to deduce that it may belong to the same period of Memling's work. We have seen that as

going abroad with the King; and Donne is on duty at Calais in the service of Hastings on 8 June 1475 (*ibid.*, p. 551).

[49] Rymer, *Foedera* XII (1711), p. 43.

[50] *Letters and Papers illustrative of the Reigns of Richard III and Henry VII*, ed. J. Gairdner (Rolls Series 1861), I, p. 15.

[51] In the appointment of Sir Richard Carewe as lieutenant of the castle of Calais in 1510 – see *Letters and Papers, Henry VIII*, I, i, second edition, pp. 195 f., no. 414(59) – it is specified that he is to hold the post 'in the same form as Sir John Donne or Anthony Browne'; also *ibid.* I, ii, p. 1102, no. 2484(29): 'as held by Sir John Donne and Sir Anthony Broun'. Since sureties for Sir Anthony Browne's safe keeping of the castle of Calais were recorded on 15 February 1497 (*Cal. Close Rolls 1485–1500*, p. 298, no. 1006), Sir John Donne's term of office may have ended about that time. On Donne's presence at Calais in the early 1490's, see Rymer, *Foedera* XII, pp. 431, 453; also *Letters and Papers, Henry VIII*, II, p. 2207: Bishop Fox recalling the time before the siege of Boulogne (October–November 1492) 'when his company, except Sir John Donne and Sir John Turberville,

had returned to England'. (Sir John Turberville was treasurer of Calais from 1490 to his death in 1502.)

[52] *Letters and Papers, Henry VIII*, V (1880), ed. Gairdner, no. 1283. Letter from John Bunolt of Calkewell to his brother Thomas, Calais 2 September 1532: he has got lodgings at Calais for Thomas Cromwell. It 'is the house that was to our aunt the lady Donne, in the most wholesome street in Calais'.

[53] The fact that nothing in particular is known about Sir John's religious affiliations suggests that they were conventional. Although some friars at the Hospital of St. John (see below, page 33 note 24, with reference to Adriaen Reyns) seem to have favoured the *devotio moderna*, which had also adherents in England (see R. Lovatt, 'The *Imitation of Christ* in Late Medieval England', *Transactions of the Royal Historical Society* XVIII, 1968, pp. 97–121), there is no reason to suppose that either the Hospital as a whole or Sir John Donne and his family had a marked preference for such an ardent and inelegant form of devotion. For some of the cults and customs officially associated with the Hospital see *Inventaire des archives de la ville de Bruges*, ed. L. Gilliodts-van Severen, I–VIII

late as 1480 it is quite possible that the Donnes had only one child, their daughter Anne. An upper limit is here again provided by the York collar with Edward IV's personal badge, which would have been worn until 1483, but hardly after the accession of Richard III.

No doubt, the two triptychs are so closely related in style as well as in subject matter that they are not likely to be many years apart. But can we be certain which came first? To ask that question is to answer it: Were the figures in one of Memling's most ambitious works copied from a small altarpiece made for Sir John Donne, the treatment of which has been described by Friedländer as 'thin, anaemic and dry'? Or was the chief altarpiece of the Hospital of St. John at Bruges repeated in a more modest form for the private pleasure and use of a distinguished foreigner, attached to the two St. Johns as his personal name-saints? Surely the second is the more probable assumption – though for my part I am inclined to think that Friedländer exaggerated the 'thin, anaemic and dry' appearance to get over the awkward disparity of dates.

In the background of the left wing of the Donne triptych, half hidden by a marble pillar, lurks a homely member of the middle class, in a red cap and with a purse at his belt (fig. 10), stylized as the only 'onlooker' of the scene. 'I consider it certain', wrote Friedländer, that this 'is a self-portrait',[54] and he drew attention to the corroborating fact that St. John the Baptist, behind whom the presumed painter had taken up his lonely post, was the painter's name-saint as well as the donor's.[55] Dating the picture to 1468 and finding that Memling looked here 'about thirty-five',[56] – he also suggested 'between thirty and forty',[57] – he concluded that Memling was born about 1433. But on the occasion of the Memling Exhibition at Bruges (1939), Friedländer revised his opinion and decided that Memling 'was not born much before 1440'.[58] The face that had looked to him between

(1871–82); *Indexes*, ed. E. Gailliard, IX–X (1882–5), particularly X, pp. 227 f., s.v. 'Hôpital Saint Jean'.

[54] *Von Eyck bis Bruegel*, p. 56.

[55] *Die altniederländische Malerei* VI, p. 14.

[56] *Von Eyck bis Bruegel*, loc. cit.

[57] *Die altniederländische Malerei*, loc. cit.

[58] 'The Memling Exhibition at Bruges', *The Burlington Magazine* LXXV (1939), p. 124. Whether the change in Friedländer's view was caused entirely by the collective effect of the paintings he saw exhibited, or, to some small degree, by a re-examination of the documents is not revealed. It may be inferred, however, that if

Parmentier had not discovered in the previous year (see below, page 29 note 5) that Memling was registered as a citizen of Bruges in 1465, which presupposes that he was then about twenty-five years old, the birth-date of 1440 would perhaps not have come so readily from Friedländer's pen. That Memling could not have been born much earlier follows from the fact that at his death, in 1494, his three sons were under age (Weale, *Hans Memlinc*, p. 12). There is much to be said for Friedländer's conclusion (*loc. cit.*) that Memling worked as a 'Geselle' at Brussels until 1464 and that 'he became an independent master at Bruges at the age of about twenty-five.' (On

thirty and forty years old would now have to look about twenty-eight, if
not twenty-six. Fortunately, if the date of the picture is advanced to about
1480, the man can continue to look close to forty. But if this is Memling,
what can we make of a number of similar interlopers in other pictures:
the shepherd looking through the window at the *Adoration of the Magi* in
the Bultync panel at Munich or in the *Adoration* in Madrid (fig. 12); or
the odd bearded onlooker in the same position in the Floreins altarpiece
at Bruges, dated 1479 (fig. 11)?[59] Apart from being bearded, this individual
looks appreciably older than the man in the red cap (fig. 10); and that
would be awkward for my thesis. My answer would be that at least one
shepherd looking on was as necessary for an Adoration as an ox and an
ass and that none of these is a self-portrait. The historical and stylistic
grounds for preferring 1480 to the late 1460's are in any case far too strong
to be upset by so flimsy a train of reasoning as that provided by a hypothetical Memling's hypothetical beard. To end this argument with a fresh
hypothesis: since the man in the red cap wears his purse as if it were an
attribute (fig. 10), it would not be unreasonable to recognize in him the
steward of the Donnes' household. A similarly placed figure looking in on
the saintly assembly of the St. John's altarpiece at Bruges (fig. 35), which
corresponds to the Donne triptych in so many other respects, was identified
some years ago as the Hospital's 'gauger'; for in a small scene further to the
left the same personage is seen gauging the wine delivered in barrels from an
impressive crane (fig. 34).[60] As a mark of identification, the purse is surely as
good as the crane and the barrels, and equally unsuited to designate a painter.

The transfer of the Chatsworth altarpiece to about 1480 removes the
chief obstacle to a proper understanding of Memling's development as an
artist. It confines to some fifteen years before his death all the products of
his mature genius instead of scattering them in apparently haphazard
fashion over the whole period of his artistic activity. Even more important,

the questionable evidence of Marcantonio Michiel, who
thought that Memling looked sixty-five years old in a
picture that he took to be a self-portrait, see below,
page 30 note 11).

[59] The frigid enlargement in Madrid (Prado, no. 1557)
of the Jan Floreins triptych retains the onlooker at the
window (fig. 12). Friedländer dates this work 'about
1470', almost certainly ten years too early, since the
Floreins triptych, on which it depends, is inscribed 1479.
The parallel to the misdating of the Donne triptych is

obvious, and perhaps not accidental. As evidence of
Memling's genius, the altarpiece in Madrid cannot count
for much, although to reject Memling's share in it
altogether (as proposed by Voll, *Memling*, p. xxvii; also H.
Kehrer, *Die heiligen drei Könige in Literatur und Kunst* II, 1909,
pp. 242 ff.) might be excessive, particularly in view of its distinguished provenance (from the collection of Charles V).

[60] Weale, *Hans Memlinc*, p. 37. According to Weale, the
office of 'gauger' was held at that time (1479) by the
master, Jodocus Willems (1475–88).

it should now be possible to trace, even in pictures produced under the shadow of Roger van der Weyden, the slow evolution of an individual style. The two paintings juxtaposed in figs. 38 and 39, for example, dated ten years apart, 1472 and 1482,[61] should suffice to dispose of the legend that Memling's art shows no signs of growth. Friedländer agreed with Hulin de Loo that the elegant *Annunciation* (fig. 39) was Memling's most felicitous invention.[62] The posture of the Virgin, supported by two angels while the dove of the Holy Ghost forms a halo over her head, suggests – more eloquently than any comparable representation – that this is the moment of the incarnation. It is all the more noteworthy that this inspired work, which shows what the mature Memling could achieve by meticulous elaboration, still retains, in what Friedländer regarded as an 'unexpectedly original composition', the vestiges of a Rogerian formula.[63]

Nor did Memling disguise his debt to Roger (fig. 28) when he had to compose, for one of the wings of the St. John's Altarpiece at Bruges (1479), a *Martyrdom of St. John the Baptist* (fig. 26). The brutal subject was so uncongenial to his temperament that the executioner looks like a fatuous dandy, compared with the atrocious henchman in Roger (fig. 28). However, if Roger conceived of Salome as a mannered damsel, Memling made her assume a motionless posture (fig. 29). It is surprising to find that he modelled her sleek face on an image of the Virgin (figs. 30, 31), bringing Purity and Turpitude so close together that the change-over is achieved by infinitesimal touches – a boldness unprecedented in Roger's practice. In the background, stillness pervades the landscape of the Jordan, where St. John performs the Baptism of Christ in the presence of a pellucid angel (fig. 27).

In Memling's art of portraiture, such early examples as the Portinari pair, datable about 1471 (figs. 133, 134), and such a mature work as the Nieuwenhove portrait, inscribed 1487 (fig. 152), should have shown clearly in what direction Memling's powers expanded in that genre;[64] but observation

[61] It has been suggested that the date 1472, inscribed on the upper wall in the Ottawa picture, between the canopy and the window (fig. 38), is retraced; but in that case it would presumably repeat an older inscription. The date of the *Annunciation* (fig. 39), 1482, is again not as plainly verifiable as one might wish: it was inscribed on the original frame of the picture, now replaced. Friedländer was probably right to accept both dates in spite of these reservations (*Die altniederländische Malerei* VI, pp. 25, 35; also p. 121 no. 26; p. 128 no. 64).

[62] *Die altniederländische Malerei* VI, p. 35.

[63] Compare Roger's famous *Annunciation* on the left wing of the Columba Altarpiece, Alte Pinakothek, Munich, no. 102. Even in such a rebarbative genre as the crowded religious panorama, of which figs. 70 and 71 represent successive phases (details, figs. 72–6 as against 77–81), a certain growth of freedom is demonstrable: the documentary and stylistic evidence for dating these two paintings ten years apart (1470 and 1480) is set forth below, page 40 note 50).

[64] The intimate 'devotional diptych', in which a worshipper is joined to a Madonna (figs. 151–2), is again a

was deflected by an error of judgement supported by the misdating of the Chatsworth triptych. Until 1927 the admirable portrait of a man holding a coin (fig. 141), and supposedly recognizable as an Italian not only by his features, but by the otherwise unmotivated presence of a palm tree in the background (fig. 142a), was believed to represent Charles the Bold's Italian medallist Niccolò Spinelli, who seems only to have spent a year (1467–8) in the Low Countries.[65] Although the style of this painting is closely related to that of Memling's maturest portraits (figs. 147 ff.), the inference that it *must* have been painted in 1467–8 was un-questioningly drawn for many decades – until Hulin de Loo proposed to substitute for Spinelli another Italian medallist, Giovanni Candida, who was in Charles the Bold's service from 1472 onwards, and from 1477–9 in that of the Duke's daughter Mary of Burgundy.[66] This solution of the problem found little favour since Candida's appearance is known[67] and was not very like the man in Memling's portrait. Besides, as Friedländer pointed out,[68] a distinguished Italian medallist would have displayed not a coin of Nero, but an example of his own skill: This therefore was not a medallist but a collector of Roman coins, a nameless Italian antiquary,[69] –

form taken over from Roger and enriched by Memling with imaginative detail that Roger did not envisage: see Hulin de Loo, 'Diptychs by Rogier van der Weyden', *The Burlington Magazine* XLIII (1923), pp. 53–7; XLIV (1924), pp. 179–89; Panofsky, *Early Netherlandish Painting*, pp. 294 f., 479 note 16. In re-assembling some diptychs by Roger that had been dismantled, Hulin laid down two rigid rules that were then adopted by Panofsky, who furthermore added a third rule to complete the system. As these 'Three Laws' have bedevilled the study of Memling's portraiture, it is necessary to list and question them here: (1) If the bust or half-length portrait of a man represents him 'with hands joined in the act of prayer', this is 'proof' that the picture originally belonged to a devotional diptych or triptych. (2) In a diptych the por-trait invariably occupies the sinister wing, the donor *facing to his right* in worshipping the Virgin and Child. (3) If such a worshipper is represented *facing to his left*, the image *must* be the dexter wing of a triptych whose sinister wing would then be occupied by another por-trait, presumably of the sitter's wife *facing to her right*. – Laws (2) and (3) are contradicted by a well-preserved diptych in the Louvre by Jan Gossart (nos. 1997–8: devotional portrait of Jean Carondelet) where both the inscription and the posture of the Infant Christ make it cer-tain that the donor *facing to his left* is the only worshipper. Our figs. 143 and 144 may well belong to the same class. Concerning Law (1), it is open to question whether

a portrait like our fig. 147, in which the gesture of the hands is conceived as a pious attribute, is part of a diptych as necessarily as, say, our fig. 152.

[65] Friedländer. *Von Eyck bis Bruegel*, p. 58.

[66] Hulin de Loo, 'Le Portrait du Médailleur par Hans Memling: Jean de Candida et non Niccolò Spinelli', *Festschrift Friedländer*, pp. 103–6.

[67] See G. F. Hill, *A Corpus of Italian Medals* (1930), pl. 134 no. 823; also text, pp. 213, 244.

[68] *Die altniederländische Malerei* VI, p. 42.

[69] It is unfortunate for Friedländer's otherwise so cogent remark that the coin displayed – a sestertius of Nero – is much too common an antiquarian object to qualify as a collector's emblem. Perhaps the man was not primarily a numismatist, but only happened to be a Nero – like a certain surgeon, Leonardo di Girolamo del Nero, whose portrait, on a medal by Niccolò Spinelli (Hill, no. 1058), has a certain family resemblance with Memling's sitter. As may be seen from Milanesi's index to Benedetto Varchi's *Storia fiorentina* (1857), Nerone or Neroni was a common Italian name. In 1458 a Simone di Nerone was in partnership with the Medici. If a Palma Nerone could be found in the Italian colony at Bruges, this would of course fit the picture completely. In the meantime this speculation is as gratuitous as any other. The coin is rendered, incidentally, with such clarity that Dr. Kraay was able to identify the mint: it is Lyons (*Lugdunum*), not Rome. This means that the specimen belongs to an

in which case an early date becomes unnecessary, as on the grounds of style it is unlikely.[70]

That Memling should have produced an isolated example of his maturest style of portraiture as early as 1467–8, three or four years before the Portinari portraits, ought never to have been entertained. What allowed it to be, and also deprived the portrait's relegation to a later date of much of its force, was the existence of the Chatsworth altarpiece, securely dated before 1469 and thus providing evidence of Memling's early maturity. Even so circumspect a scholar as the late W. H. J. Weale, who, from the 1860's onward, did perhaps more than any other archivist to explode legendary tales about Memling,[71] began the second chapter of his classic book, *Hans Memlinc*,[72] with the following sentence: 'The earliest pictures which can with certainty be ascribed to Memlinc are the portrait of Nicolas Spinelli and the triptych of the Donne family.'

issue particularly common north of the Alps (fig. 142b).

[70] The reservations of the preceding note do not invalidate this conclusion.

[71] Weale's most important contributions are listed in the Chronological Bibliography prefixed to his *Hans Memlinc* (1901), pp. xv-xxiv.

[72] *ibid.*, p. 13.

PART II

The Authorship of the Danzig Last Judgement

THE Danzig *Last Judgement* (figs. 40–68) is a work of critical importance for the study of the Rogerian school of painting in the Low Countries during the decade or so following the master's death. (Roger died in 1464, and the altarpiece was shipped in 1473.) Although Memling was singled out for mention by Vasari as Roger's best-known pupil, there were certainly others, including at least one of Roger's sons; and the master's influence can be detected in the work of Petrus Christus (who died, apparently at Bruges where he had long been settled, about 1472) and of Dieric Bouts, as well as in the products of various nameless and mostly inferior masters. That this *Last Judgement* was painted by an artist who was not only familiar with Roger's works, but had been deeply influenced by them and probably also by him, is immediately obvious. We need, however, to remember that by itself that does not point conclusively to Memling. What must make us hesitate to disallow his claim to be its author is its confident attribution to him and to him alone on grounds of style by most if not all modern scholars. It may be best if we first examine it closely without bothering too much about who painted it.

The triptych when closed (fig. 41) displays on the outsides of its wings kneeling figures of the donor and his wife,[1] before two round-headed

[1] For the identification of the donors as Angelo di Jacopo Tani (chief agent of the Medici bank in Bruges before Tommaso Portinari) and his wife Catarina, daughter of Francesco Tanagli, see A. Warburg, 'Flandrische Kunst und florentinische Frührenaissance' (1902), reprinted with additions in *Gesammelte Schriften* I (1932), pp. 192–6; 373–6; compare also below, pages 24 ff., 34 f. Warburg gives a pungent account of the Hanseatic piracy by which this altarpiece, destined for Florence and shipped *via* England in 1473, reached the Marienkirche in Danzig. The Hanse and England were at war. Since the well-stored Florentine vessel, registered in Bruges as the possession of Duke Charles's councillor Tommaso Portinari, had sailed under the Burgundian flag while carrying a valuable cargo of alum and of much other merchandise to England (an inventory of 1473 is published in *Hanserecesse 1431–1476*, ed. G. von der Ropp, VII, 1892, pp. 115 ff., no. 41; another, compiled for the court sitting at Malines on 5 August 1496, in *Inventaire des archives de la ville de Bruges*, ed. L. Gilliodts -van Severen, VI, 1876, pp. 410–17, no. 1262, which gives the complete court ruling), the culpability was perhaps not exclusively on the side of the raider. For more than twenty years Danzig refused to pay compensation, even after the state court at Malines had decided in favour of the Italians (see Gilliodts-van Severen, *loc. cit.*). Finally, on 5 November 1499 the city of Bruges, rather than see their fine commerce with the Hanse disturbed, offered to buy the Florentine claim for 12,000 florins, payable in six annual instalments (*Cartulaire de*

niches in which stand a Virgin and Child under a Rogerian circular canopy,[2] and a St. Michael flourishing a sword at a couple of mocking devils. The light comes from the left-hand side, as it does in the Last Judgement scenes within (figs. 45, 51). Donors, coats of arms and floor are in colour. The rest of these outer shutters is painted in *grisaille* to represent stone. There is a certain resemblance between this Virgin and Child and that in the 1472 Ottawa panel, with the Virgin standing and the Child clothed (fig. 38). The St. Michael is largely a *grisaille* version of the same saint holding the scales in the central panel of the triptych (fig. 40). The tile-pattern on the floor is simpler than those that Memling usually displays.

Angelo Tani in a robe of black velvet lined with brown fur does not wear his heart or even his brains on his sleeve. Yet it is an arresting if enigmatic face (fig. 42). It is easy to believe that he furthered the interests of his firm with determination and skill.[3] His wife, born Catarina Tanagli, for all her wealth of pearls and her red hair, has a look of discontent (fig. 43). As an essay in portraiture this has little in common with the almost perpendicular Gothic elegance of Lady Donne, but the difference may have lain more in the subjects than in the painter's treatment of them.[4]

The first impression one derives from looking at the central panel is the

l'ancienne estaple de Bruges, ed. Gilliodts-van Severen, II, 1905, pp. 320–3, no. 1315). That the acceptance of that offer by the Florentines, dated 27 November 1499, was officially transmitted to the Hanse is shown by the fact that the best copy of the original document has survived in Lübeck (Staatsarchiv, *Varia*, no. 267c, quoted by Warburg, *Gesammelte Schriften*, p. 373). The people of Danzig thus acquired formal possession of the *Last Judgement* as part of a handsome gift from the people of Bruges. For further evidence on this *cause célèbre* see A. Reumont, 'Di alcune relazioni dei Fiorentini colla città di Danzica', *Archivio storico italiano* XIII (1861), pp. 37–47; G. von der Ropp, 'Zur Geschichte des Alaunhandels im 15. Jahrhundert', *Hansische Geschichtsblätter* (1901), pp. 117–36; also *Hanserecesse* VII, p. 2, with documents listed in Index p. 874, s.v. 'Portinari'; F. Prims, 'Het schip van Portunari, 1473–1498', *Antwerpiensia* XII (1939), nos. 12 f., pp. 76–89; and finally W. Drost, *Das Jüngste Gericht des Hans Memling in der Marienkirche zu Danzig* (1941), pp. 8 ff.

2 Exactly the same canopy, also in *grisaille*, appears in a typical product of Roger's workshop, a shutter with an *Ecce Homo*, now in the Bob Jones University Art Gallery, Greenville, South Carolina (see Friedländer, *Die altniederländische Malerei* II, 1924, p. 120, no. 87a;

also Exhibition Catalogue *Flanders in the Fifteenth Century*, Detroit Institute of Arts, 1960, no. 11, pp. 87–9, with illustration). The form of the canopy is related to the tent-shaped setting of Roger's *Medici Madonna* in Frankfurt; compare also the 'tent of heaven' in compositions ascribed to the Master of Flémalle (Panofsky, figs. 210, 231). An inept imitator of Roger and Memling doubled the motif on a pair of shutters, where these celestial canopies crown an *Expulsion from Paradise* (reproduced in *Les primitifs flamands: collections d'Espagne*, ed. J. Lavalleye, I, 1953, no. 46, pl. LIII).

3 The sharp silhouette of his primly cut robe, with pointed angles (fig. 41), is more in the style of Van der Weyden or Van der Goes (fig. 136) than of Memling. Altogether the portrait has a determined and energetic twist uncommon in Memling.

4 The possibility should also not be ruled out that this strikingly Italianate portrait was not painted from life but from a drawing taken in Italy. Tani did not marry until 1466, two years after he had left Bruges for Florence (see below, pages 25 f.), and it is doubtful whether his wife would have accompanied him on the extremely troublesome and hectic business visits that brought him back to Bruges after that date.

easy mastery with which this crowded scene is organised (fig. 45). The gold background edged with greenish-grey frills of cloud in the upper half of the Judgement contrasts with the spatial depth of the terrestrial landscape below: the bare green countryside in which the dead rise from their graves stretches away in well-managed perspective to the blue hills on the horizon. There is a similar contrast between the hieratic attitudes of the Judge with his celestial companions and the wild scenes in which the damned abandon themselves to despair on the right side of the panel's lower half. The gesticulating apostles, like a row of deaf-mutes in the front of the dress-circle, may recall Memling's stiff figures of the two St. Johns; but the mass of writhing lost souls is something new. The significant thing is that what reminds us most of Memling are things which he derived with little change from his reputed master. There can, I think, be no doubt of the Rogerian character of the upper group of figures: the Judge, the Virgin and the Baptist backed by the twelve apostles, the angels with the instruments of the Passion and even, though less so, the trumpet trio suspended between earth and sky, all these seem to echo van der Weyden's *Last Judgement* at Beaune (figs. 44, 50), unveiled in 1451. If the Danzig apostles seem almost a caricature of Memling's later manner, it is interesting to find the same stiff gestures in the Community of the Saints at Beaune. The Virgin in particular is more Rogerian than anything we have hitherto seen in Memling. On the other hand the shallow and diminutive world in which Roger's dead emerge from holes in the earth rather than from graves, is markedly unlike the extraordinary impression of depth achieved by the Danzig picture where in the middle distance angel and devil struggle for the possession of a soul.[5]

Let us concentrate for a few minutes on the central scene in which the souls are being weighed (fig. 45). In the Beaune *Last Judgement* (fig. 44) St. Michael is staring straight before him. Here his eyes are lowered, with

[5] It may also be noted that while Roger lined the wings of St. Michael with a formal pattern derived from peacock-feathers (fig. 44), the painter of the Danzig altarpiece has made the peacock-feathers look real: they hang down from the ends of the wings like glittering tails (fig. 45). As a bird emblematic of the afterlife, the peacock rivalled the glory of the phoenix (see L. von Sybel, *Christliche Antike* I, 1906, pp. 171 f., pls. ii, iv; Mrs. H. Jenner, *Christian Symbolism*, 1910, pp. 149 f.; C. R. Morey, *Early Christian Art*, 1942, figs. 28, 85). St. Augustine believed 'the flesh of a dead peacock to remain always sweet and without putrefaction' (*De civitate Dei* XXI, iv, with full account of a successful experiment by which he had tested the theory in Carthage); but he drew from this example the awful conclusion that man's body and soul may last forever in the fires and tortures of Hell. In the Danzig *Last Judgement* the realistic feathers hanging down from St. Michael's wings look sinister enough to convey that threat (fig. 68) as counterpart to the celestial promise.

an expression of care and sad benignity, more like a guardian-angel tha n an angel of justice (fig. 40). The head of the saved soul in Michael's scales has caused considerable speculation. The identification of the face as that of Tani's successor, Tommaso Portinari, though widely accepted, seems to me difficult to credit.[6] To represent a living man and business colleague naked, and undoubtedly saved, on an altarpiece destined for public worship is an eccentricity which would have laid Tani open to ribald comment, particularly as it was not unknown that the relations between the two men were far from friendly.[7] However, in view of the widespread tendency to hold on to this ridiculous fiction, a relevant fact may here be cited. The head is admittedly among the worst-preserved parts of the painting, having severely suffered from rough treatment by the restorer Christoph Krey in 1718, and again by the restorer Christian Xeller in 1851. The latter's report on this particular passage is of a disarming honesty:

'The head of the just man in the scales was much the worst case of all; it had to be supplied completely after the previous head, already over-painted by a later hand, had rapidly dissolved in the course of cleaning. A little sheet of silver appeared underneath on which the design had been laid out. I used that foundation as suitable to the character, and I succeeded in imitating the previous head so faithfully in colour and expression that no one would take it for a new painting.'[8]

In short, the head is modern (fig. 67), and that may explain why it stands out from the rest 'like a portrait' (fig. 52).[9] There are also iconographic reasons why this figure cannot recall a real man: it represents

[6] A list of opinions in favour of this proposition, compiled by J. Bialostocki, *Les primitifs flamands: les musées de Pologne* (1966), pp. 64, 74, includes Warburg, Friedländer, Fierens-Gevaert, Panofsky, Van der Elst and the compiler himself.

[7] See below, page 25.

[8] The complete report, issued by Xeller in 1852 as part of a little treatise, *Über das Jüngste Gericht in der Pfarrkirche in Danzig*, is reprinted in Bialostocki, *op. cit.*, pp. 117 f. Since Xeller was a close friend of H. G. Hotho (on whom see below, page 23), a remark by Hotho on the physical state of the painting, about eight years before Xeller was called to restore it, may be taken to reflect Xeller's own opinion at that time: 'Der Kopf des Gerechten auf der Wagschale . . . ergibt sich sogleich als neues Machwerk . . . . Leider scheint der alte Kopf

darunter verloren' (Hotho, *Geschichte der deutschen und niederländischen Malerei* II, 1843, p. 144; compare also J. D. Fiorillo, *Geschichte der zeichnenden Künste in Deutschland und den vereinigten Niederlanden* II, 1817, p. 224 note a). On three further restorations, in 1934, 1947, and 1955, see Bialostocki, *op. cit.*, p. 89.

[9] Remarkable is Friedländer's insistence on listing this nineteenth-century head among the authentic portraits of Portinari by Memling: 'Memling placed Portinari's head on one of the resurrected figures in the Danzig *Last Judgement*, the man in the scales of the archangel' (*Die altniederländische Malerei* VI, p. 39). And again (p. 116): 'The naked man in St. Michael's descending scale bears the well-known features of Tommaso Portinari, whom Memling portrayed several times'.

only *part* of a soul, the part that had lived a virtuous life and is now being weighed against the sinful part. To interpret it as a whole soul would make nonsense of the weighing.[10]

Immediately to the left and behind the weighing of souls, an anxious pair have emerged from their graves (fig. 53) and are waiting for their turn to enter the scales. In Vienna there are panels of Adam and Eve (fig. 69) attributed to Memling where the Eve is not unlike the woman in the Danzig *Last Judgement* (fig. 68). Kenneth Clark has picked her out as 'a typical Gothic nude of the 15th century.'[11] But Adam is far less 'Gothic', and the men in the *Last Judgement* even less so. That is to say, Memling shared with the Danzig artist a preference for 'idealised' Gothic female nudes and for naturalistic, accurately observed male nudes. But so did van Eyck and others of the Bruges school.

Among the resurrected in the Danzig *Last Judgement* some of the faces are so strongly marked that there can be little doubt they were drawn from the living model (fig. 66): but since the most striking are repeated several times (figs. 53, 54), and transferred from the blessed to the damned without hesitation (cf. figs. 53 and 54 with fig. 55), it is clear that they were intended as types: the method is the same as in the Beaune altarpiece, where Roger stressed the resemblance between the blessed and the damned: they are of one stock.

The saved move off in the direction of Heaven, looking back and over their shoulders at the Judgement scene (fig. 52). Unlike Roger's (fig. 50), they are numerous and tightly packed (figs. 51, 61, 62). The Danzig painter took a more hopeful view of man's chances than his master. Nothing could be more characteristic of Roger's severity than that the scales held by St. Michael descend on the side of the sins (inscribed PECCATA): the event signifies perdition, and the angel's eyes, wide open on the spectator, convey a threat (fig. 44). In the Danzig Altarpiece, where the angel has benignly lowered his eyes, the weighing is interpreted propitiously: the piety outweighs the sin (fig. 45).[12] To account for this difference by postulating two contrary types of *psychostasis*[13] is unnecessary and confusing.

---

[10] See M. P. Perry, 'On the Psychostasis in Christian Art', *The Burlington Magazine* XXII (1912), pp. 94–105; (1913), pp. 208–18.

[11] Kenneth Clark, *The Nude* (1956), p. 18.

[12] No doubt the terms of the commission (discussed below, pages 24 f.) have some bearing on this feature. A donor dedicating an altarpiece to St. Michael as his patron-saint would expect the Saint to be pictured in a propitious moment.

[13] Panofsky, *Early Netherlandish Painting*, p. 272.

The weighing is conducted in both cases on the same principle, but spelling out damnation in the one case, salvation in the other. Roger was closer to the *dies irae*, whereas the painter of the Danzig *Last Judgement*, although competent enough in the depiction of Hell, seems to have found his real subject in the Heavenly City.

The steps of Heaven are crowded with the saved (figs. 61 ff.) and as, after shaking hands with St. Peter, they receive back their clothes, a pope, two cardinals and at least one bishop are revealed (fig. 61). The portal through which they pass is an architectural curiosity, with its animated statues and musicians' galleries. Above the tympanum in which God the Father sits in majesty surrounded by the evangelists is a roundel with the creation of Eve, the start of the whole human story here again ended in Paradise: *et erunt duo in carne una*. The ground in the central panel is green but no flower grows there. Only where the earth touches the steps of glass leading to Heaven do they spring up and bloom. Here are dandelions, orange lilies, scarlet poppies, violets and columbines, painstakingly observed and carefully rendered.

If Heaven is crowded Hell is hardly less so (figs. 51, 58). Above, the last trump fills what would otherwise be a blank corner and some of the damned seem to have been levitated among the smoke and flames to fill the middle distance with incident (fig. 56), while the foreground is a mass of clutching, falling figures. The infra-red photographs throw some interesting light on the way the artist sketched out his first design and modified it slightly in the final execution (figs. 63, 67). Infra-red prints of Memling's other supposed works do not often show such changes so clearly.

This impressive triptych with its 112 square feet of painted surface and its 150 figures must have taken its creator several years to execute.[14] What are we to think? Is this a Memling? Convinced that the Donne triptych was an undoubted product of the 1460's, recent scholars such as Friedländer, Hulin and Baldass have not hesitated to answer: yes. But we can no longer feel certain. It is true that many of the figures are suggestive of Memling's style, but have they anything more in common with his known works than a shared Rogerian ancestry? In the period immediately

[14] There is evidence that Memling needed more than four years to complete the triptych of St. John's at Bruges (see below, page 34 note 25).

after Roger's death in 1464 Memling was nearer to his main source of inspiration and teaching. But the notable fact about the Danzig *Last Judgement* is the respect in which it departs both from the Rogerian norm and from Memling's known practice. Can those tortured and contorted damned and athletic devils who drag them down to Hell be from the same hand as those elegant and immobile martyrs in the St. John's altar-piece and the placid scenes, all tension relaxed, over which the Virgin and Child calmly preside in all the pictures that we know to be his? Can a different subject so modify an artist's normal mood? If this is by Memling, not only did he achieve maturity early – though no other comparable work of that date can be identified – but he brought off something that he was never (so far as we know) to attempt again. This would not only be his most ambitious undertaking, but one in which he displayed – and exploited with confidence and facility – talents which he later so conspicuously lacked. It is as if he had dared to exceed his proper range when Roger's influence was still strong and afterwards lapsed into a placidity of feeling natural to himself – and satisfactory to his many customers. I must confess that I do not find this assumption particularly likely. The vividness and animation of parts of the *Last Judgement* seem wholly foreign to what we know for certain about Memling's art.

But what other reasonable explanations are there? Roger himself was dead; and in any case there are too many elements in the picture which are completely un-Rogerian, mixed with those which have an obvious origin in Rogerian practice. Was there any other artist working in those years in or near Bruges who was more capable than Memling of these departures from Rogerian tradition? There was Petrus Christus; and it is undoubtedly true that scholars have been unsuccessful in finding much painted by him that they can assign to the last two decades of his life. But a *Last Judgement* by him, signed and dated 1452,[15] would seem to rule him out. There is, however, a panel in the Louvre of the *Fall of the Damned into Hell* (fig. 59) which may possibly stand comparison with the right wing of the Danzig triptych (fig. 58).[16] The figures show the same knowledge of anatomical form, in particular the two figures in the right foreground. On the other

[15] Staatliche Museen, Berlin-Dahlem, no. 529B.

[16] W. Schöne, *Dieric Bouts und seine Schule* (1938), pp. 98 ff.; Edouard Michel, *Catalogue raisonné des peintures* *flamandes du XVe et du XVIe siècle Musée du Louvre* (1953), pp. 22 f.; no. 1904A.

hand, the unusual mastery of an intricate composition which is the most striking quality in the Danzig *Last Judgement* seems here far less evident. This panel, together with one of the *Fountain of Life* in the Museum at Lille (fig. 60), is attributed by most authorities to Dieric Bouts the elder of Louvain and regarded as being one of the wings of a lost *Last Judgement* commissioned in 1468 for the Town Hall at Louvain and completed in 1472. The chief difficulty about this identification is that the Louvain triptych was 6 feet tall and these two panels are less than 4 feet and do not appear to have been cut down. But if they are by Bouts, then the Louvain school may be thought either to have influenced the Danzig master or to have assisted him; if they are not by Dieric Bouts or his sons (already painting in the early 1470's), then whoever painted them must be associated with the Danzig master. At least this panel demonstrates that there was someone, probably not Memling, who could have had a hand in our *Last Judgement*.

It is necessary to arrive at some conclusion, but it had better be a tentative one. That is easy, since there is clearly no justification for confidence. I must confess that despite the resemblances and despite the difficulty of attributing the picture to another known artist, I am unable to convince myself that this is the unaided work of the youthful Memling, his master-piece in both senses of that word. On the other hand the attribution cannot entirely be ruled out and it is possible that he had a hand in it. My conclusion, therefore, would be School of Roger, showing affinities with Bouts and Memling but possibly by a third unidentified master: the Master of the Danzig *Last Judgement*: an admission of defeat.

EDITOR'S NOTE

The boldness of doubting an attribution to Memling that has had the unqualified support of Friedländer, Hulin de Loo, Panofsky, Puyvelde, Voll and Winkler (to name only a few) might well seem excessive – were it not for a fact unmentioned and perhaps unremembered by these authors: that it was not until 1843 that Memling's name first became attached to the Danzig *Last Judgement*. The attribution was proposed by H. G. Hotho (the editor of Hegel's *Aesthetics*) in the second volume of his *Geschichte der deutschen und niederländischen Malerei* (pp. 128–45). Although widely accepted at the time, Hotho's thesis met with some opposition, particularly from the formidable Carl Schnaase, native of Danzig, who drew attention to the paradox that if this was an early work by Memling, it displayed a skill in monumental design, combined with an expressive use of anatomical science and a virtuosity in diabolical genre, such as Memling was never to reveal again (see *Geschichte der bildenden Künste* VIII, 1879, pp. 252–61). Less radical were Ernst Förster's objections (*Denkmale deutscher Kunst* IX, iii, 1864: 'Das Danziger Bild', pp. 11 f.): Having observed that the general conception of the *Last Judgement*, and also some parts of the execution, were closely related to Roger van der Weyden, he concluded that this work, so confidently ascribed entirely to Memling, was most probably commissioned from Roger's workshop, perhaps while Memling was Roger's apprentice. Although this would date the commission before Roger's death, which occurred in 1464, it would not exclude the possibility that the triptych was completed by Memling a few years after, as suggested by the date inscribed on a slab in the central panel: ANNO DOMINI [MC]CCCLXVII. The inscription runs along the edge of the slab, on three sides (fig. 68), and Förster's reading of it is unquestionably right. (On the fourth side, not discussed by Förster, is a small fragment of script that looks like IC IAC, possibly IS IAS, in which case it could be the remnant of the name IS[A]IAS, referring to Isaiah xxvi, 19: 'vivent mortui', a canonical prophecy of the resurrection. There is little to recommend the current reconstruction [H]IC IAC[ET], on a tomb from which the dead are rising!).

The further progress of the debate is well summarized by W. Drost, *Das Jüngste Gericht des Hans Memling in der Marienkirche zu Danzig* (1941), pp. 14–17, except that Weale's *Hans Memlinc* (1901) is mistakenly included among the books that interpret the Danzig altarpiece as an 'organic part' of Memling's output. In fact, Weale referred to that work as the most important painting that had been *erroneously* ascribed to Memling (p. 71); and far from recanting that opinion (as claimed in *Les primitifs flamands: les musées de Pologne*, ed. J. Bialostocki, 1966, p. 83), he reaffirmed his reservations in *The Burlington Magazine* XV (1909), p. 314. A list of other dissenting views, regretfully compiled by Bialostocki (*op. cit.*, p. 84), includes a fresh discussion by M. W. Brockwell in *The Connoisseur* CIV (1939), pp. 258 f., and a doctoral dissertation by P. Trzeciak (1960). One thing will be clear from this rapid survey: to doubt Memling's authorship is not so rare.

Some insufficiently explored iconographical features, which are connected with the donor's name and his history, may possibly prove that Förster's view, published in 1864 (see above), came close to the truth. The donor's name was Angelo Tani (*not* Jacopo Tani, as Voll, Friedländer, E. G. Troche, and even Thieme-Becker, misname him: Jacopo was Angelo's father). Since Angelo is but a shortening of Michelangelo, it is clear why the angel Michael plays such a prominent part in this altarpiece – not only as the pivotal figure of the *Last Judgement*, but as the donor's personal intercessor on the outer wings. Admittedly, it could be argued, in comparing the giant angel in Danzig (fig. 45) with its prototype in Beaune (fig. 44), that it was only too typical of Memling's workmanship that, faced with the commission of a *Last Judgement*, he would borrow the grand design from Roger van der Weyden (repeating the posture of the Christ quite literally, even retaining the curious disposition of his cloak on the rainbow, see figs. 48, 49), and then refine the handling in a Laputan style by imagining that the laws of optics would remain so neatly intact on the Day of Judgement that the resurrection of the dead could be seen mirrored in St. Michael's polished armour (fig. 46), and the heavenly host, with St. Michael below, appear reversed in the globe under Christ's feet (fig. 47). To introduce such optical surprises into a devotional context is not uncharacteristic of Memling: witness the mirror-image in the Nieuwenhove diptych (fig. 151), which shows the seated Virgin unbecomingly from behind, and the donor also in reverse. However, if in the present case the painter projected his *Kleinmeisterei* into an austere design appropriated from Roger van der Weyden, it is virtually certain, in view of the emphasis placed on St. Michael, that the use of a Rogerian prototype was in this instance the donor's rather than the painter's choice and formed an essential part of the commission. By providing that St. Michael should be seen first on the outer wings, next to the Madonna, painted in *grisaille*, and then, when the wings were opened, as the dominant actor of the sacred drama, Angelo Tani imparted to his donation the devotional stamp of a *St. Michael's Altarpiece*. And if that idea had come to him, as seems more than likely, under the impact of the huge St. Michael that dominated the *Last Judgement* at Beaune (unveiled in 1451), then the obvious course for Tani was to order his altarpiece from the same shop, particularly if the master was still alive.

When could Angelo Tani have commissioned such a large and ambitious work? Only after 1455, when he became the head of the Medici firm in Bruges, and sometime before 1465, when he was superseded in that post by his rival, Tommaso Portinari, who initiated a policy that Tani tried in vain to resist (see A. Grunzweig, *Correspondance de la filiale de Bruges des Medici* I, 1931, pp. xvi–xxxviii). Tani left Bruges for Florence in 1464 (*ibid.*, p. xvii), and although he continued to defend his interests in Bruges from afar and was even sent north by the Medici in 1467, and again in 1468–9, to see if he could avert a financial debacle in their London branch that would severely affect the business in Bruges, the differences of opinion between him and his partners proved unsurmountable in the end. In 1473 he had to admit defeat: for on 26 March of that year (*ibid.*, p. xxx; see also R. de Roover, *Money, Banking and Credit in Mediaeval Bruges*, 1948, p. 87) the Medici drew up a fresh contract that gave Tommaso Portinari, contrary to Tani's persistent advice, a completely free hand in the affairs of Bruges. In the same year Tani's altarpiece was shipped, presumably with a consignment of other belongings that he may have kept in Bruges in the vain hope of regaining the ascendancy.

In the light of these disappointments it has been suggested (cf. Warburg, *Gesammelte Schriften* I, pp. 194, 374 note) that the date 1467 inscribed on the *Last Judgement* was perhaps not meant to be read as the date of the painting, as assumed by Förster, Waagen, Weale and many others, but that it commemorates a particularly troublesome moment in the donor's career, when the affairs at Bruges were threatened with bankruptcy because of their connexion with London.[17] Would that not have been the moment to vow an altarpiece to the protecting saint? Be that as it may, a cryptic inscription, the true meaning of which remains to be guessed, would defeat the purpose of an *ex voto*. As it stands, the inscription is better read, in the old-fashioned way, as giving the year in which the painting was finished: for it was a fairly common pictorial practice, particularly among Flemish painters of that period, to introduce such dates, as if they were carved, on some pieces of stonework within the pictures, a wall or a sill, as in fig. 150; a slab (close to St. Michael, near the centre of the *Last Judgement*) would obviously do as well.

If it is admitted, on the evidence of the inscription, that the painting was completed in 1467, and that a triptych of that size and intricacy would have taken four or five years to produce, the date of the commission would be about 1462–63, when Tani was at the zenith of his career in Bruges. Since Tani married a distinguished Florentine in 1466 (at the age of fifty), and his wife (thirty years his junior) is represented opposite to him on the outer wings, the triptych would have been finished very shortly after the marriage, and this is supported by the fact that none of the three daughters is represented. One of them, Margherita Maria Romola, was born 8 June 1471 (Warburg, p. 374) – a conclusive *terminus ante quem*, corroborative of the date inscribed on the painting. Furthermore, considering that Tani's wife was named Catarina, the absence of a St. Catherine from the outer wings, where St. Michael appears as Angelo's name-saint, is not only surprising in itself, but it leads to an unexpected grouping of the figures: Angelo Tani, instead of appearing, as was the custom, below his patron saint, has ceded that place to his wife – out of deference to two other customs: that a husband, when portrayed next to his wife, must appear on her right, but that St. Michael, if placed next to the Virgin, would necessarily have to remain on her left. The upper and the lower zones, if taken separately, conform each to normal etiquette; but when combined, they suggest a makeshift arrangement, possibly due to the fact that in 1466, when Angelo married, the triptych was virtually complete; and having been conceived as a St. Michael's Altar-

[17] Warburg referred to this crisis as *die Affäre Canigiani* (*Gesammelte Schriften*, p. 374) because it was connected with large loans advanced to Edward IV by the London branch of the Medici bank, then directed by Gherardo Canigiani. Tommaso Portinari was providing in Bruges for equally adventurous loans to Charles of Burgundy, whereas Tani got involved in these affairs against his will. The names of all three appear as creditors – 'Tommasio Portinari, Angelo Tani and Gerard Caniziani' – in a warrant from Edward IV to the exchequer (discovered by Dr. Harriss in the Public Record Office, E 404/74/1/45, dated June 1468), in which John Donne figures among those who had stood surety (in his case to the extent of 200 marks) for a loan totalling 10,000 pounds. If this was part of the dowry of Margaret of York's marriage to Charles the Bold, it can be said without exaggeration that Portinari had been financing the wedding on both sides. In Florence, Piero de' Medici must have formed the same opinion of these transactions as Tani: for in a contract drawn up with Portinari in 1469 (Florence, Archivio di Stato: *Carteggio Mediceo avanti il Principato, filza 84, carta 32 bis, ter*) the lending of money to crowned heads and courtiers is criticized as being more risky than profitable, whereas the Medici house wishes to conduct its business in a form that will 'preserve its property, its credit and its honour', without enriching itself by gambles (Warburg, p. 199, also p. 193 note 4.) Unfortunately for Tani, Piero de' Medici died in December 1469, and his successor, Lorenzo the Magnificent, preferred political pageantry to business: he sided, at least for the time being, with Portinari.

piece, it could not accommodate a prominent St. Catherine without unhinging the liturgical programme. (An X-ray has revealed that the two coats of arms were painted first in inverse positions, that of Tani under St. Michael, and that of his wife below the Virgin: see Bialostocki, *op. cit.*, pp. 61, 79, pl. ccxxix. While it would be tempting to quote this fact in support of the view that in the original plan Tani was meant to appear on the side of St. Michael, the possibility cannot be ruled out that the exchange of place, being confined in the X-ray to the coats of arms, was no more than a trivial workshop error corrected by the repainting.)

At least one conclusion may be drawn with confidence: Friedländer was mistaken in his belief that the date of shipment (1473) must have followed very closely on the date of the painting (*Altniederländische Malerei* VI, p. 116, also p. 15). Considering that Tani's residence in Bruges came to an end in 1464, and that he returned from Florence only for sporadic visits and under exceedingly trying circumstances, the sheer grandeur and costliness of the object suggest that he commissioned it before these troubles began. As Memling established himself as a citizen of Bruges in 1465, a year after Roger's death (see below, page 29 note 5), the painting may well have received the finishing touches in his studio, but if it was completed there in 1467, the date when it was begun falls almost certainly within the last years of Roger's life, when Memling is generally thought to have been his apprentice (see Hulin de Loo, 'Hans Memling in Rogier van der Weyden's Studio', *The Burlington Magazine* LII, 1928, pp. 160 ff.). If all these circumstances are taken into account, and held against the internal evidence of the painting, they point to a conclusion very similar to Förster's: that this triptych is a posthumous issue from Roger's workshop, with Memling's hand very much in evidence.

PART III

The Character and Reputation of Memling's Art

WHEN Hans Memling died at Bruges on 11 August 1494 a contemporary diarist noted that he was 'then held to have been the most skilful and most excellent painter of the whole Christian world.'[1] The judgement may have contained some obituary exaggeration, but it cannot be dismissed as narrowly parochial. For the parish was still, even in 1494, a great cosmopolitan city. When Memling established himself there in 1465, Bruges, though economic historians can now see that its decline had begun, seemed to contemporaries to be at the height of its wealth and splendour. Though cut off more and more completely from the open sea, in spite of vast and expensive dredging operations, by the silting up of its only waterway,[2] and hard-pressed by the expansion of the English cloth-industry,[3] Bruges in the last third of the fifteenth century was still full of accumulated wealth: it was still the place where the agents of the great foreign banking-houses in the Low Countries resided, the resort of all who had business with them, of diplomatic missions, travellers and political exiles. It was among the well-to-do members of this cosmopolitan mercantile community that Memling was to find the bulk of his known patrons. His art appealed less to the visionary or the courtier than to the narrow, sober and 'realistic' bankers and men of trade. No more improbable story could easily have been invented than the late tradition that assigned him as a mercenary to the service of Charles the Bold and pictured him as a

[1] *Fragments inédits de Romboudt de Doppere: chronique brugeoise de 1491 à 1498*, ed. H. Dussart (1892), p. 49, relating to the year 1494: 'Die XI. augusti Brugis obiit magister Johannes Memmelinc, quem praedicabant peritissimum fuisse et excellentissimum pictorem totius tunc orbis christiani. Oriundus erat Magunciaco, sepultus Brugis ad Aegidii.' The writer was chapter-clerk of St. Donatian's, Bruges. That he knew Memling has been inferred from the fact that on 21 October 1489 he certified the deposition of certain relics, associated with St. Ursula and the eleven thousand Virgins, in the shrine decorated for that purpose by Memling and donated to the Hospital of St. John in Bruges (*ibid.*, p. iii note 1).

[2] On the silting of the Zwim and the measures taken against it from 1470 onwards see L. Gilliodts-van Severen, *Bruges port de mer, étude historique* (1895), pp. 44–186. Compare also *Cartulaire de l'ancienne estaple de Bruges*, ed. Gilliodts-van Severen II (1905), p. 341, no. 1327.

[3] *ibid.*, p. 294, no. 1281; pp. 298 ff., no. 1290 (ordinance against importation of English cloth, issued on 8 April 1494 and amplified on 18 January 1495).

disabled veteran from the fields of Granson and Morat, nursed back to health in the Hospital of St. John at Bruges and repaying his benefactors by decorating their church.[4] It would be nearer the truth to maintain that he was a burgess painting for burgesses. There is no need to be prejudiced against him on that account.

The record of his life is all too brief. The first occasion of which we know was on 30 January 1465 when as son of Herrmann and native of Seligenstadt he was admitted a citizen of Bruges.[5] To qualify for admission he must then have been at least 25 years of age. His birthplace was on the Main between Aschaffenburg and Frankfurt in the temporal and spiritual dominions of the Elector of Mainz. He came, that is to say, from a region associated with a very different artist, Grünewald, his junior by some 25 years. In the sixteenth century he was still remembered as Hans from Germany; the village of Mömlingen, from which he probably took his name, lies a few miles to the south of Aschaffenburg; but not even the most chauvinistic of art-historians have been able to detect a peculiarly Teutonic element in his style. Nothing for certain is known about his training as a painter, nor indeed anything about his movements before he arrived, a fully-fledged master, in the city where he was to spend the remaining thirty years of his life. But Vasari describes him as the pupil of Master Roger[6] and since Van der Weyden died in June 1464 after long residence in Brussels[7] it is reasonable to believe that Memling's settlement at Bruges followed, and was a result of, the elder painter's death. How long he had been at Brussels – whether, for instance, he had received the whole of his artistic training in Roger's studio – is doubtful, although Roger's imprint on his work cannot be questioned. The next thing we know about him is a negative: when in the summer of 1468 many artists from all over the Burgundian lands were collected in Bruges to execute the elaborate

[4] J. B. Descamps, *La vie des peintres flamands* I (1753), pp. 12 f.; cf. [W. H. J. Weale], 'L'école de Bruges et les Annales Archéologiques de Paris', *Le Beffroi* I (Bruges 1863), pp. 65–71, particularly p. 66: 'Il a plu à Descamps, ce ridicule écrivain français, d'estropier les noms de nos artistes et de fausser les faits et les dates de leur vie.' Fromentin, in 1876, regretted the exposure of Descamps: 'Malheureusement, paraît-il, et quel dommage! ce joli roman n'est qu'une légende à laquelle il faut renoncer. D'après l'histoire véridique, Memling serait tout simplement un bourgeois de Bruges' (*Les maîtres d'autrefois*, final chapter).

[5] R. A. Parmentier, *Indices op de Brugsche Poorterboeken* I (1938), p. xxvi; II, p. 630, s.v. 'Mimnelinghe', with illustration p. (157), pl. II. See also M. W. Brockwell, 'A Document concerning Memling', *The Connoisseur* CIV (1939), pp. 186 f.

[6] *Vite*, ed. Milanesi, I (1878), pp. 184 f.; II, p. 566; VII (1881), p. 580; cf. also Lodovico Guicciardini, *Descrittione di tutti i Paesi Bassi* (1567), p. 98.

[7] A. Pinchart, 'Roger de la Pasture dit Van der Weyden', *Bulletin des commissions royales d'art et d'archéologie* VI (Brussels 1867), pp. 442 f., 450 f.

decorations needed for the festivities which followed Duke Charles's marriage with Margaret of York, Memling does not seem to have been employed.[8] Between 1470 and 1480 he himself took a wife Anne, to judge from her father's name (de Valkenaere) of Flemish stock. About the same time he purchased three houses in the best quarter of the city, including one described as large and of stone; and his assessment for taxation placed him among the 247 wealthiest citizens of Bruges, of whom only 140 were taxed higher than he.[9] His marital life was cut short by the premature death of his wife, which occurred before 10 September 1487: and in 1495, a year after his own death, his three sons were still under age.[10] What was taken to be a self-portrait was seen in the house of Cardinal Grimani at Venice in 1521;[11] the subject was described as 'fat and red-faced'. And that is all.

The names of some of Memling's patrons have been preserved. Among them were men prominent in the government of Bruges and drawn from its leading families. Pieter Bultync, a prosperous member of the Tanners' Guild, donated to their chapel one of the most poetic paintings by Memling, a sacred panorama of Christ's epiphanies, centred in the journey and adoration of the Magi (figs. 71, 77 ff.),[12] with portraits of the donor, his wife and their son (figs. 80, 81).[13] Willem Moreel, of Italian descent

[8] His name does not figure in the list of payments published by L. de Laborde, *Les ducs de Bourgogne, Preuves* II (1851), pp. 293–382; see also Laborde, *Essai d'un catalogue des artistes originaires des Pays-Bas ou employés à la cour des ducs de Bourgogne aux XIVe et XVe siècles* (1849), p. 46: 'ce nom ne figure pas dans les comptes'.

[9] Weale, 'Documents authentiques concernant la vie, la famille et la position sociale de Jean Memlinc', *Journal des beaux arts et de la littérature* (Brussels 1861), pp. 21–55, 196; also *Hans Memlinc* (1901), p. 10.

[10] *ibid.*, p. 12.

[11] *Notizia d'opere di disegno nella prima metà del secolo XVI . . . scritta da un Anonimo di quel tempo* [i.e. Marcantonio Michiel], ed. Jacopo Morelli (1800), p. 75: 'In casa del Cardinal Grimano: . . . El retratto a oglio de Zuan Memelino ditto è di sua mano istessa, fatto dal specchio; dal qual si comprende che l'era circa de anni 65, piuttosto grasso che altramente, e rubicondo.' The fairly strong evidence that Memling lived only to the age of about 54 (see above, page 11 note 58) does not necessarily discredit the writer. In judging the age of a Northern face, portrayed in a Northern painting of an earlier period, an Italian might excusably err by ten years. But while it would be futile to speculate whether or not this painting, now lost, was really by Memling, let alone a self-portrait, the fact that it was so regarded by a Venetian in 1521, who expressed some surprise at the lack of refinement in the face, shows that by that time Memling had become a titbit for *cognoscenti*. See also below, note 33, on a supposed Memling (a diptych) owned by Bembo. In Grimani's collection the presumed self-portrait was one of four portraits ascribed to Memling, in addition to *molti quadretti de Santi* and a portion of the illuminations (now definitely dissociated from Memling) in the famous Grimani Breviary (*ibid.*, pp. 75 ff.).

[12] The pageant of the Magi gave Memling the chance to regale the Tanners, for whom the picture was painted, with a stylish display of leather jerkins, boots, saddles and all sorts of decorated trappings worn by the horses (figs. 78 f.). The king bending his knee before the divine Child uncovers a magnificent boot (fig. 71).

[13] Weale, 'Inventaire du mobilier de la Corporation des Tanneurs de Bruges', *Le Beffroi* II (1865), pp. 264–74, with the text of an inscription copied from the original frame, now lost, of the Bultync altarpiece (p. 265) saying that 'in the year 1480 this work was given to the Corporation of the Tanners by Pieter Bultync, son of Josse, tanner and merchant, and by his wife, Katelyne, daughter of Godevaert van Riebekes'; see also Weale,

(Morelli), who belonged to the corporation of merchant-grocers, twice burgomaster of Bruges, with a notable record of civic resistance to the French as well as to Maximilian,[14] had himself and his wife portrayed by Memling in a pair of intimate devotional pictures (figs. 92, 93) and also, with their large family, as donors of a triptych for the chantry chapel founded by Moreel in the Church of St. James (figs. 82–91). Whether Jan du Celier, another merchant-grocer, is to be associated with a somewhat debatable diptych is not certain,[15] but there can be no doubt that a third member of the same corporation, Jacob Floreins, commissioned from Memling an ambitious altarpiece, including the portraits of his nineteen children (figs. 94–97), which became a sad memorial to the plague.[16] Martin van Nieuwenhove, a future town-councillor (1492) and burgo-master (1497), was portrayed by Memling at the age of twenty-three (1487) in a justly famous diptych (figs. 151 f.).[17] Finally, Memling's friend and

Hans Memlinc, pp. 23–32. The painting remained in the chapel of the Tanners' Guild until 1764. In 1827 it was bought by the King of Bavaria, Ludwig I, with the whole collection of the brothers Boisserée, who had acquired it in 1813: see correspondence with Goethe in *Sulpiz Boisserée*, ed. Mathilde Boisserée, II (1862), pp. 25–30.

[14] Weale, 'Généalogie de la famille Moreel', *Le Beffroi* II (1865), pp. 179–96, s.v. Guillaume Moreel IV (pp. 181 ff.); also *Inventaire des archives de la ville de Bruges*, ed. Gilliodts-van Severen, *Index* (Gailliard) IX, p. 109, s.v. 'Moreel, Guillaume', with particular reference to his public role. On the Moreel triptych, dated 1484, see Weale, *Hans Memlinc*, pp. 40–4, 96 f.; also A. Janssens de Bisthoven, *Les primitifs flamands: Musée Communal des Beaux-Arts, Bruges* (1959), pp. 90–103, pls. CXCVII–CCXXXVII. In 1802 Friedrich Schlegel, accompanied by the Boisserées, admired this painting in Paris (*Gemäldebeschreibungen aus Paris und den Niederlanden*, reprinted in Schlegel's *Sämtliche Werke* VI, 1846, pp. 48 f.), where it had been taken in 1794 by the French occupation forces. It was returned in 1816 (see below, note 36). Schlegel qualified his praise by the observation that, as a successor of Jan van Eyck, Memling reached such heights only occasionally. The *Adoration of the Lamb* from the Ghent Altarpiece was exhibited in Paris at the same time.

[15] The name of Jan du Celier is associated as donor with a diptych in the Louvre (nos. 2027–2027a), but this is a problematic piece. According to Friedländer, 'the flaccid form may be partly due to the state of preservation' (*Die altniederländische Malerei* VI, p. 38), and he inclines to accept the painting as a 'very late' Memling, 'particularly close to the Shrine of St. Ursula'. The date of the escutcheon, on which depends the identification of the donor (Weale, *Hans Memlinc*, p. 20), has lately been

questioned by O. le Maire (see Edouard Michel, *Catalogue raisonné des peintures flamandes, Musée du Louvre*, p. 200). The diptych was reassembled in 1894 (Michel, *loc. cit.*). On the left wing is seen a free and rather insipid paraphrase (virtually a *pastiche*) of Memling's *Marriage of St. Catherine* in Bruges, while the right wing shows a donor kneeling under the protection of St. John the Baptist, with St. George and St. John the Evangelist in the background. Contrary to Memling's custom, the landscapes in the two wings are not continuous. On a comparable painting in the Metropolitan Museum of Art, New York (no. 14.40.634, at one time in the possession of Sir Joshua Reynolds), see Erik Larsen, *Les primitifs flamands au Musée Métropolitain de New York* (1960), p. 119, fig. XX, who considers both paintings to be workshop adaptations derived from the *Mystic Marriage* in Bruges.

[16] Weale, *Hans Memlinc*, pp. 50–2, 101. This important work, which came from Spain to France and is now in the Louvre (no. 2026; see Michel's catalogue, *op. cit.*, pp. 201 ff.), was completed after the donor, Jacob Floreins, had died during the plague of 1489–90 (which struck also many of his children): his wife appears dressed as a widow. She was Spanish, of the Quintana-duena family. On leaving Bruges after her husband's death she must have taken the altarpiece with her to Spain, where General d'Armagnac is said to have found it in 1809. The fact that she has chosen St. Dominic for her protector (fig. 95), whereas her husband is introduced by his name-saint, St. James, suggests that she may have retired to a Dominican convent, perhaps the house to which one of her daughters (seen near the right edge of the painting) belonged.

[17] Weale, *Hans Memlinc*, pp. 44–6, 98; also M. Guil-laume-Linephty, *Hans Memling in the Hospital of St.*

neighbour, Willem Vrelant the miniaturist, who was a founding-member of the Stationers' Guild, presented an altarpiece of the Passion to their chapel,[18] though whether this survives in the gallery of Turin (fig. 70) may be matter for dispute.[19] The fact that the Stationers' altarpiece had shutters, which are notably absent from the panel in Turin, does not speak necessarily against it, since shutters often get detached; but if an inventory of the Guild, dated 20 December 1499, is correctly quoted as saying that the donors' portraits were painted on the shutters,[20] this would conclusively rule out the picture in Turin, where the portraits of the kneeling donors (as in the Bultync altarpiece, figs. 71, 80 f.) are incorporated in the panel (figs. 70, 75 f.).[21]

John at Bruges (1939), pls. 9 f., where the diptych is reproduced with the original frames, inscribed: HOC · OPUS · FIERI · FECIT · MARTINUS · D̤ · NEWEN-HOVEN · ANNO · DM̄ · 1487 · (on the side of the Virgin and Child); continued ANº · VERO · ETATIS · SUE · 23 · (on the side of the donor).

[18] On Willem Vrelant the miniaturist, and his style of book-illumination, see F. Winkler, *Die flämische Buchmalerei des XV. und XVI. Jahrhunderts* (1925), pp. 9, 71, pls. 35–7; Paul Durrieu, *La miniature flamande au temps de la cour de Bourgogne* (1927), pp. 20 f., pls. X–XIV; L. M. J. Delaissé, in *La miniature flamande: le mécénat de Philippe le Bon*, Exhibition Catalogue (Brussels 1959), pp. 99–123, pls. 41, 47, 48; also *A Century of Dutch Manuscript Illumination* (1968), pp. 74 ff., 94. Some useful notes on Vrelant's person, particularly in relation to Memling, are appended to A. Schestag, 'Die Chronik von Jerusalem', *Jahrbuch der kunsthistorischen Sammlungen des Allerhöchsten Kaiserhauses in Wien* XX (1899), pp. 195–216. The altar-panel painted by Memling for the Stationers' Guild was a picture of the Passion, presented by Vrelant in 1478, at a guild-meeting attended by Memling as a guest. At the order of the guild, and at their expense, the panel was equipped with shutters commissioned from Memling (see *Le Beffroi* IV, 1872–3, pp. 299, 336), and in this form it was installed in their chapel two years later (1480). The picture was sold in 1624, and its later history is uncertain (cf. Weale, *Hans Memlinc*, p. 105).

[19] The painting now in Turin, of doubtful provenance, is an unquestionable Memling, and of the same subject and size as Vrelant's donation (see Weale, 'Memling's Passion Picture in the Turin Gallery', *The Burlington Magazine* XII, 1908, pp. 309–11, with further literature). Although filled with over twenty episodes comprising more than two hundred figures besides horses and dogs (figs. 70, 72 ff.), the painting is only 22 inches high and 36 inches wide, so that its effect is akin to miniature painting, also in the architectural staging of the many

scenes. These bear some resemblance to Vrelant's own way of constructing towns out of cubicles that recall the 'mansions' of the Miracle Plays (on which see J. Mesnil, *L'art au nord et au sud des Alpes à l'époque de la Renaissance*, 1911, p. 101). However, none of these affinities of style, size and subject are sufficiently unique to prove beyond doubt that this small picture is actually the panel painted for Vrelant, particularly as another small Memling, also of the Passion, was commissioned directly for Italy and seen by Vasari. That this is more likely to be the painting in Turin was suggested by Warburg: see below, note 21. – As an oddity it may be noted that A. von Wurzbach (*Niederländisches Künstlerlexikon*, s.v. 'Vrelant') found the Turin painting to be so clearly the work of a miniaturist that he ascribed it to Vrelant himself, even though, as an illuminator registered with the Stationers' Guild, Vrelant was not permitted to paint in oil (see *Le Beffroi* IV, pp. 244 f.). One of the consequences of Wurzbach's theory, and drawn by him with commendable logic, is that if Vrelant painted the Turin *Passion*, he must have painted the Bultync altarpiece as well!

[20] C. Aru and E. de Geradon, *Les primitifs flamands: la Galerie Sabauda de Turin* (1952), p. 16.

[21] According to Warburg's theory ('Flandrische Kunst und florentinische Frührenaissance', *Gesammelte Schriften* I, pp. 197 ff., 376 f.), endorsed by Friedländer (*Die altniederländische Malerei* VI, pp. 15, 21 f., 132 no. 34), also by Mesnil (*L'art au nord et au sud des Alpes*, p. 27), the painting now in Turin would have been in Italy since the end of the fifteenth century: it would in fact be the *quadretto piccolo* by Memling, representing the Passion, which, according to Vasari, had been commissioned by the Portinaris for the Hospital of S. Maria Nuova in Florence, whence it passed into the collection of Duke Cosimo de' Medici. Here Vasari had the opportunity of studying it and of informing himself about its history (*ed. cit.* I, pp. 184 f.; VII, p. 580). Since Memling's portraits of Tommaso and Maria Portinari (figs. 133 f.) show a strong resemblance with the pair

Like the guilds, the religious houses received paintings by Memling from their members, some of whom belonged to the same families. Jan Floreins, for example, a brother of Jacob, the merchant grocer, joined the community of St. John's Hospital in 1472. The triptych of the *Adoration of the Magi* (fig. 14), which he gave in 1479, represents him as a modest friar (fig. 13),[22] ten years before the troubled period in which he held the office of spiritual master.[23] The name of another friar of the same house, Adriaen Reyns (figs. 15, 20), is connected with a more austere donation of 1480, a small stark triptych of the *Lamentation* (figs. 17–21), as hard as the anvil held by St. Adrian (fig. 18), and barely dulcified on the outer wings by two amiable anchorites, St. Mary of Egypt and St. Wilgefortis (figs. 22 f.).[24] In contrast to this sparse, ascetic piece, there is a touch of festive splendour about the *Mystic Marriage of St. Catherine* (fig. 35), more correctly a *Holy Conversation* since the ring received by St. Catherine from the Child is treated as one of her attributes and does not render her

of donors represented on the panel in Turin (figs. 75 f.), this view has found general acceptance, at least for the time being. The Vrelant-hypothesis, although well-argued by Weale in its own terms (above, note 19), suffers from three disadvantages: First, that no portraits of Willem Vrelant and his wife seem to have survived so that it is not possible, as in the case of the Portinaris, to compare them with the donors' portraits in Turin. Secondly, that Vrelant is said to have been a man of advanced age when he commissioned Memling's painting for the Stationers' Guild, so that he and his wife ought to look much older than the pair of donors in the Turin picture. Thirdly, that there is some ground for supposing that in the work commissioned for the Stationers' Guild the portraits of the donors appeared on the shutters (above, note 20).

[22] Weale, *Hans Memlinc*, pp. 32–5, 97. The original frames of the triptych (reproduced in Guillaume-Linephty, *Hans Memling in the Hospital of St. John at Bruges*, pls. 3–5) carry on the outside the initials of the donor, I. F., and his coat of arms; on the inside the following inscription, divided between the three panels: DIT · WERCK · DEDE · MAKEN · BROEDER · IAN · FLOREINS / ALIAS · VANDER · RIIST · BROEDER · PROFFES · VANDE · HOSPITALE · VAN · SINT · · IANS · IN · BRVGGHE · ANNO · M CCCC LXXIX ·/ OPUS · IOHANIS · MEMLING. The figure 36, indicating the donor's age, appears carved into the stone of the left arch, just next to his head. That the youth standing behind him is a portrait of his younger brother, Jacob, (as claimed by Weale, *Hans Memlinc*, p. 34), would be easier to believe if we did not have Jacob's portrait ten years later as father of nineteen children

(fig. 95). The youth could be a nephew, perhaps Jacob's eldest son, who was destined for the priesthood and appears in the family altarpiece dressed in cassock and surplice (fig. 96).

[23] In 1489 all the other brethren (the sisters proved tougher) were removed by pestilence, and Jan Floreins found himself alone, at the head of a community that needed replenishing. Having imprudently admitted four servants and several convalescent inmates of the Hospital as brothers, he soon became involved in disputes with an unruly crowd of men without vocation, who even tried to rouse the sisters against him. In 1497, after failing to obtain episcopal support from Tournai, he threw up the struggle and resigned. He died a simple brother in 1504.

[24] Weale, *Hans Memlinc*, pp. 64, 98. On the inner panels the unexpectedly stiff appearance of St. Barbara (fig. 19) and the *rigor mortis* in the body of Christ (figs. 17, 21) are not signs of clumsiness on the part of the painter but of his close attention to a devotional style imposed by the *imitatio Christi*, so strangely foreshadowed in the legend of St. Wilgefortis (fig. 22): she was believed to have carried the imitation of Christ in her ardent meditations to such a pitch that she was physically transformed into Christ's bearded image: whereupon she was made to suffer his martyrdom. Hence the cross as her attribute in Memling's image, and also the beard, but this monstrous feature appears subdued by comparison with the rugged look of St. Mary of Egypt (fig. 23), semi-nude, to show that she is clothed in her hair, and carrying the three loaves that nourished her in the wilderness. To make these two frightful anchorites look kindly is a feat not easily to be ascribed to anyone but Memling.

much more prominent than St. Barbara, or the two St. Johns. The triptych was presented for the High Altar of the St. John's Hospital by the four members who are portrayed on the outer wings, kneeling below their patron saints; Antonis Seghers with St. Anthony Abbot; Jacob de Kueninc with St. James (fig. 24); Agnes Casembrood with St. Agnes; and Clara van Hulsen with St. Clare (fig. 25).[25] The triptych must have been regarded as the most sumptuous donation to the Hospital – until the advent of that expensive piece of church-furniture, the *Shrine of St. Ursula and the Eleven Thousand Virgins,* swarming with figures painted by Memling (figs. 98–108). At one end Memling managed to squeeze in the two donors – presumed to be Josina van Dudzeele and Anna van den Moortele – kneeling beside a tall image of the Virgin and Child in a small Gothic oratory (fig. 103).[26] The sisters probably knew the story of the abbot who obtained the body of one of the Virgins and promised to keep it in a shrine of silver upon the altar of his abbey. Then, when he gave her only a shrine of oak she rose up and walked away back to Cologne. The heavily gilt reliquary decorated by Memling made certain that that would not occur at Bruges.[27]

Of Memling's foreign patrons a few at least can be identified: Tommaso Portinari (fig. 133), the Medici's factor in Bruges;[28] his predecessor Angelo Tani (fig. 42), if we admit that Memling had a hand in the Danzig altarpiece;[29] Benedetto di Pigello Portinari (fig. 150), Tommaso's nephew and a

[25] Weale, *Hans Memlinc,* pp. 35–40, 97. The frame of the central panel is inscribed: OPUS · IOHANNIS · MEMLING · ANNO · M·CCCC·LXXIX, accepted by Friedländer as 'glaubhaft' (*op. cit.* VI, p. 117 no. 11); see also above, page 4 note 23. Coremans, Sneyers and Thissen (*op. cit.,* pp. 83 f., 95) correctly define the picture as a *Holy Conversation.* As one of the donors portrayed on the shutters (Antonis Seghers) died in 1475, Memling must have worked on this commission at least four years.

[26] Weale, *Hans Memlinc,* pp. 46–50, 98; Friedländer VI, pp. 37, 121 no. 24. Romboudt de Doppere (see above, note 1) was the notary who drew up the Act of Translation of the Relics. The shrine was consecrated on 21 October 1489. It is the only work by Memling mentioned in Karel van Mander's *Schilderboeck* (1604, fol. 204ʳ), apparently in deference to the judgement of Pieter Pourbus, who 'never tired of praising the workmanship' when he saw the reliquary displayed on feast days. An example of mid-nineteenth century sentiment, which really made of this object what Friedländer called it ('der bevorzugte Liebling unter Memlings Werken') is to be

found in C. Delapierre and A. Voisin, *La Châsse de Sainte Ursule* (Brussels 1841), with line engravings by Charles Onghena.

[27] Nevertheless, when the shrine was officially opened recently, no relics were found in it: they had been stolen (see Guillaume-Linephty, *La Châsse de Sainte Ursule,* 1958, p. 11). The story of the untrustworthy abbot is told in the *Legenda aurea.*

[28] Tommaso Portinari's commissions to Memling, of a painting of the Passion for S. Maria Nuova in Florence (probably our fig. 70, as explained above, note 21), and of a pair of portraits of his young wife and himself (figs. 133 f.), antedate by several years the famous Portinari Altarpiece by Hugo van der Goes, now in the Uffizi, which Burckhardt still saw in S. Maria Nuova (*Cicerone* III, vi, s.v.). It has been noticed that in the gaunt portrait of Maria Portinari, drawn by Van der Goes in his starkest manner (fig. 136), she wears the same jewelled necklace as in the earlier and so much more gracious picture by Memling (fig. 134).

[29] The donors of the Danzig Altarpiece, at one time believed to be Flemish or German, were conclusively

partner in his firm after its separation from the Medici;[30] the Lübeck merchant and banker Heinrich Greverade (fig. 120), for whom Memling painted an important altarpiece, possibly his last major work (dated 1491);[31] and that Welsh knight in the English king's household, Sir John Donne of Kidwelly (fig. 3).[32] In the sixteenth century some of Memling's works appear in Italian *virtuoso* collections like Grimaldi's or Bembo's;[33]

identified as Italians by Warburg on the basis of their coats-of-arms (Tani and Tanagli) and of a corresponding marriage entry for the year 1466 in the Florentine archives (*op. cit.*, pp. 192 f.); see also above, pages 16 n., 17, 24 ff.

[30] Dated 1487, Memling's devotional diptych for Benedetto Portinari (figs. 149 f.) represents him at the age of 21, when he helped to administer the wrecked Portinari fortunes in Bruges, from which the Medici had dissociated themselves in 1480. The diptych came to the Uffizi from S. Maria Nuova, without designation of the sitter (identified by Warburg, 'Flandrische Kunst und florentinische Frührenaissance', *ed. cit.*, p. 201). In this sensitive and intelligent portrait, which rivals that of Martin van Nieuwenhove in originality, the donor addresses his devotion to his name-saint, behind whom a painting of the Crucifixion appears on the wall, with Mary and St. John at the foot of the cross. To postulate in this case a central panel with the Madonna (Friedländer, *Die altniederländische Malerei* VI, pp. 37, 120 no. 23) might be redundant. If left as a diptych, the importance given to St. Benedict would resemble the role of St. Christopher in the Moreel altarpiece (fig. 87): both are seen occupying a place normally reserved for the Virgin and Child (cf. below, note 48), but surrendered here to a personal intercessor. The statuettes on St. Benedict's pastoral staff represent Samson killing the Lion and St. John exorcizing the Serpent, figures of victory over death. It may be worth noting that in the 1490's, after Tommaso Portinari's retirement, Benedetto and his brother Folco continued to defend the Portinari interests in Bruges, with partial success, as in the Danzig affair (above, page 16 note 1): see also Warburg, p. 201, on the sale for 9000 ducats of the famous Burgundian *riche fleur-de-lis,* studded with precious stones and relics, which had been retained among the securities for the fatal loans to Charles the Bold.

[31] C. G. Heise, *Der Lübecker Passionsaltar von Hans Memling* (1950), pp. vii f.; also Weale, *Hans Memlinc,* pp. 53–8, 104. On the donor's religious affiliations see below, note 47. The circumstances under which the Lübeck Altarpiece (figs. 111–30) was 'rediscovered' in the early nineteenth century by Carl Friedrich von Rumohr should help to dispel the notion (proposed by Friedländer, as quoted below, note 40, and still upheld by Heise, *op. cit.*, p. xv) that Memling was the first Netherlander to be appreciated by the German Romantics. It was in fact a fit of local patriotism that inspired the young Rumohr

(later famed for his *Italienische Forschungen*) to contribute an essay on some north-eastern German antiquities to Schlegel's periodical *Deutsches Museum* (IV, 1813, pp. 479–516: 'Einige Nachrichten von Altertümern des transalbingischen Sachsens'), in which he singled out the Lübeck Altarpiece for an extensive description (pp. 490–5). For a just estimation of this performance it must be remembered that Rumohr's estate, Rothenhausen, was located on the outskirts of Lübeck. Unaware that the painting was by Memling, he took it to be of South-German workmanship (possibly related to the elder Holbein) but declined to ascribe it to any particular master, or to explain why in this case a Southerner would have been employed in the North. The local gentry, he thought, was well portrayed in the three unpleasant characters whom we have tentatively called 'a Pharisee and two Levites' (fig. 124). Rumohr was positive that in one of them he could detect a family resemblance with the Brömbsen clan, whose faces he had studied in the Brömbsen Chapel of the Jakobikirche in Lübeck. Surprisingly, he had nothing to say of the donor, Heinrich Greverade, whose portrait (fig. 120) he mistook for a cleric. Some ten years later, still in the spirit of parochial enthusiasm, Rumohr commissioned a group of local artists to reproduce the Lübeck Altarpiece in lithographs. This work appeared in 1825 under the suggestive title: *Altargemälde der Greveraden-Kapelle im Dom zu Lübeck: Steindrucke von Carl Julius Milde, Erwin und Otto Speckter,* again without the painter's name – a further proof that in the 1820's the cult of Memling lagged far behind the popularity of the Van Eycks (on which see below, note 40). So far as attribution was concerned, Rumohr did not go much beyond C. H. von Heinecken, *Nachrichten von Künstlern und Kunstsachen* II (1769), p. 75, who had drawn attention to the Lübeck Altarpiece without venturing to determine its author.

[32] See above, pages 1–10; below pages 52 ff.

[33] *Notizia d'opere di disegno* (cf. above, note 11), p. 17: 'In casa de M. Pietro Bembo: El quadretto in due portelle de S. Zuan Battista vestito, con l'agnello, che siede in un paese da una parte, e la nostra Donna con el puttino dall' altra in un altro paese, furono de man de Zuan Memeglino, l'anno 1470, salvo el vero'. It has been supposed that a wing of that diptych, representing St. John the Baptist, is now in Munich (Alte Pinakothek, no. 115), but not only is this panel too broad for a wing (12⅝″ by 9½″), but the Baptist, if placed on the left side of the Virgin, would face in the wrong direction.

others are listed among the treasures of Margaret of Austria;[34] but the artist's original clientele, whether in Flanders, in Florence or in Lübeck, was predominantly middle-class. The only aristocratic names directly connected with his extensive output were those of James of Savoy and Anthony of Burgundy. Of both these men there exist portraits which are believed to be early copies of lost originals by Memling.[35] For the rest he catered, it seems exclusively, for the *haute-bourgeoisie* of many lands, finding among them a ready market for the products of his flourishing workshop.

His reputation was not to stand as high again until the mid-nineteenth century. His revival then is perhaps not surprising, for that was the great age of the burgher collections in Europe, when Bruges became a necessary place of pilgrimage for art-lovers.[36] The experts agreed with the people and they gushed in confident unison.[37] The difference between their aesthetic

[34] *Correspondance de l'empereur Maximilien Iᵉʳ et de Marguerite d'Autriche, de 1507 à 1519*, ed. A. J. G. Le Glay, II (1839), pp. 479 f. ('Inventaire des painctures fait à Malines'); see also 'Inventaire des tableaux, livres, joyaux et meubles de Marguerite d'Autriche . . . fait . . . en la ville d'Anvers, le 15 avril 1524', ed. L. de Laborde, *Revue archéologique* VII (Paris 1850), pp. 56 f., no. 124. An *Angel holding a Sword*, now in the Wallace Collection (fig. 109), could be a fragment from a pair of small shutters described in these inventories: both shutters were painted by Memling (*maistre Hans*) and each showed an angel (*deux feuillets dans chacun desquels il y a un ange*), one of them with a sword in his hand (*tenant l'un une épée en sa main*). The panel to which these shutters were attached was a small *Pietà* by Roger van der Weyden, but this does not mean that Memling painted the shutters as Roger's apprentice: they may have been commissioned from *maistre Hans* well after the older master's death. Since the inventories give no hint as to when and how Margaret of Austria acquired this little triptych, it is impossible to infer by whom any part of it was originally commissioned. See also Friedländer, *Die altniederländische Malerei* VI, p. 17.

[35] The portrait of James of Savoy (*ibid.*, p. 134, no. 101) is in the Öffentliche Kunstsammlung, Basle; that of Anthony of Burgundy exists in two copies (*ibid.*, no. 102, a–b), one in the Gemäldegalerie, Dresden, the other in the Musée Condé, Chantilly (our fig. 139). A further candidate for inclusion in this class is the portrait of a kneeling donor, believed to be Francisco de Royas (formerly in an Amsterdam collection, sold at Sotheby's on 29 November 1961; see L. von Baldass, *Hans Memling*, 1942, pl. 94; Friedländer, *Die altniederländische Malerei* XIV, 1937, p. 103, also in *Oud Holland* LXI, 1946, p. 19),

but the identification of the sitter is not certain, although the coat of arms is thought to be that of Royas.

[36] On 20 December 1812 (cf. above, note 13), Sulpiz Boisserée reported to Goethe that 'apart from the main works of Hemmling [= Memling] in Bruges' his brother had not seen much of importance on his last excursion to Flanders, the main objects of attraction being then in Paris. To judge by Stendhal's denunciation of the fascinated Parisian crowds that assembled every Sunday at the Musée Napoléon in front of *une croûte de l'école allemande*, in fact the Danzig *Last Judgement* (see *Lettres . . . sur Haydn, . . . Mozart, . . . Métastase*, 1814, p. 136: the letter in question is dated 1809), Napoleon may have done as much as the brothers Boisserée to bring Flemish art of the fifteenth century to the attention of the *bourgeoisie*. No doubt, Bruges owed much of its nineteenth-century fame to the restitutions negotiated in 1815, on which see J.-P. Sosson, *Les primitifs flamands de Bruges: apports des archives contemporaines, 1815–1907* (1966), pp. 15 f. On 3 January 1816 (p. 53) the *Van der Paele Madonna* by Jan van Eyck, the *Moreel Altarpiece* by Memling, the two *Cambyses* pictures by Gerard David and Michelangelo's *Madonna of Bruges* returned in triumph from Paris. It is perhaps excusable that in 1812 Melchior Boisserée had not found quite enough to see.

[37] The following titles and dates may suffice: Mrs. Jameson, *Sacred and Legendary Art* I (1848), p. 129, fig. 56; Dante Gabriel Rossetti, *Sonnets*, first published in *The Germ* (1850), p. 180: 'A Virgin and Child, by Hans Memmeling, in the Academy of Bruges'; also 'A Marriage of St. Katherine, by the same in the Hospital of St. John at Bruges'; Crowe and Cavalcaselle, *The Early Flemish Painters* (1857); Weale, *Catalogue du Musée de l'Académie de Bruges* (1861); also *Bruges et ses environs*

prejudices and ours is strikingly illustrated by Fromentin's unargued assertion that Roger van der Weyden's historical importance was 'above all to have left among his works a unique masterpiece – I mean a pupil who was called Memling.'[38] The Bruges master was for the second time on the crest of the wave.

And now his stock has slumped once more. The critical judgements of recent art-historians have been consistently deflationary. To Sir Martin Conway 'a single picture by Memling is delightful, but a collection of several monotonous. . . . Memling was the Perugino of the North.'[39] Above all Friedländer has used his great authority to bring about a steady depression of Memling's aesthetic rank: 'of the famous Netherlanders of the fifteenth century', he wrote in 1916, 'Memling least deserves the title of a master who furthered and increased the estate of art (*Förderer und Mehrer des Kunstreiches*). His imagination was not sufficiently bold, nor his perception sufficiently keen, to forge ahead, like Goes or Geertgen, either along the common road or on irregular byways. Compared with the older painters he is an epigone, and his images seem vacuous in their opaque cool colours. . . . But despite all changes of appreciation his amiable and well-balanced nature will continue to gain him friends.'[40] Twelve years later the

---

(1862); G. Rodenbach, *Bruges-la-Morte* (1892). When Ruskin explained to his father how much he valued the friendship of Burne-Jones, he said that his genius was 'as strange and high as that of Albert Dürer or Hans Memling' (12 August 1862, quoted in E. T. Cook, *The Life of John Ruskin* II, 1911, p. 44).

[38] Eugène Fromentin, *Les maîtres d'autrefois* (1876), of which the final chapter returns (after the Flemish and Dutch masters of the seventeenth century) to 'cette étonnante période comprise entre les débuts des Van Eyck et la disparition de Memling'. Roger is dismissed as an irrelevant offshoot: 'Van der Weyden n'a d'autre importance historique que de tenter à Bruxelles ce qui s'accomplissait merveilleusement à Gand et à Bruges' (here quoted from the 15th edition, 1906, pp. 419, 421).

[39] W. M. Conway, *The Van Eycks and their Followers* (1921), p. 230.

[40] *Von Eyck bis Bruegel*, p. 62. Friedländer went so far as to imagine that, thanks to the innocuous character of Memling's art, his popularity in the nineteenth century not only surpassed but *antedated* that of Jan van Eyck: 'At a time when fifteenth-century art in general, and that of the Netherlands in particular, was felt to contradict the canons of beauty, Memling was able, as the first Netherlander, to pass the gateway guarded by aesthetic prejudice.' However, on closer inspection, this view may prove to be an historical illusion. In so far as the classicist reaction to the Netherlandish 'primitives' can be judged by opinions prevalent in Weimar, such petulant remarks on Jan van Eyck as appeared in Goethe's *Farbenlehre* (III, v, 24: 'Geschichte des Kolorits seit Wiederherstellung der Kunst', written for Goethe by Johann Heinrich Meyer) were not accompanied by a recognition of Memling; and when Goethe recanted in 1816 and extolled 'das Unbegreifliche der Eyckischen Vortrefflichkeit' (*Kunst und Altertum* I, 1816, pp. 166–76), he referred to Memling only as one of the 'estimable artists', *schätzenswerte Künstler*, who formed the succession to Jan van Eyck (p. 181). That classicists, with only a limited interest in Memling, were in fact passionate admirers of the Van Eycks is shown by Schinkel's correspondence (*Aus Schinkels Nachlass*, ed. A. von Wolzogen, II, 1862, pp. 182 f.: report to the Prussian minister Von Altenstein, 6 August 1816, in which Canova's enthusiastic opinion of the Van Eycks is quoted; also *Aus* [Schinkels] *Tagebüchern und Briefen*, ed. Günter Meier, 1967, pp. 49–53: letter to the classicist sculptor Christian Rauch, 14 November 1816, calling for an 'apotheosis' of the Van Eycks). For further evidence see Johanna Schopenhauer, *Johannes van Eyck und seine Nachfolger* (1822), a popular work of two volumes, compiled in Weimar by the philosopher's mother; G. F.

judgement had become rather more severe: 'Memling's narrative flows along in soft ripples, gently leading toward the blessed isles of redemption, gliding over the surface of terrors while abiding by festive occasions. The slight and shallow stream is not obstructed nor dammed by that concentrated kind of observation, by that intense, intimate sympathy with visual fact, by that minute articulation of formal peculiarities – in short, by any of those characteristic exertions that invest Netherlandish panelpainting with depth, density, weight and rigour. Well-groomed and clean like the people in the foreground, the country greets us from afar, parklike, summery, with winding roads, white horses, calm waters, swans, pleasant and comfortable houses and blue hills at the horizon – an idyllic homeland where the weather is always fine. Memling is neither an explorer like Jan van Eyck nor an inventor like Roger. He lacks both the passion of seeing and the fanaticism of belief.'[41]

Heartily endorsing this criticism Professor Panofsky adds the crushing rider that Memling is 'that very model of a major minor master', a Felix Mendelssohn among painters: 'he occasionally enchants, never offends and never overwhelms. His works give the impression of derivativeness, not because he depended on his forerunners (as even the greatest did and do) but because he failed to penetrate them.'[42] For these and other reasons, as Friedländer put it, 'his creations appeared pale and dim to the following generations, until the Romantics in the nineteenth century rediscovered this thornless flower.'[43]

These criticisms are not so much unfounded as beside the point, for they take no account of what Memling was trying to do. Certainly there is nothing particularly disturbing about his art, but then neither his religious beliefs nor his aesthetic system required it to disturb; and it is difficult to see why that should be the sole or even the main purpose of all 'great' art. I

Waagen, *Über Hubert und Jan van Eyck* (1822); also Alexander von Humboldt, *Kosmos* II (1847, pp. 81, 128 note 16, with reference to lectures dating back to 1828); and many others. Perhaps the museum best known to Friedländer would be best suited to disprove his thesis. Fifteen years before the first recognizable Memling or near-Memling (1836) was to enter the Picture Gallery at Berlin (our fig. 146), the Flemish purchases from the Solly Collection (1821) showed a predominant taste for Van Eyck. Even the Boisserées were no exception to this general rule. Although they had shared Schlegel's delight in a Memling they had seen together in Paris as early as

1802 (see above, note 14), in their purchasing plans 'our great Van Eyck' (in fact, a Roger) took precedence over the Memlings that they began to acquire in 1813 to 'support' their proudest possession (see *Sulpiz Boisserée*, as quoted above, note 13). It was in fact not until the mid-century (cf. our note 37) that Memling's popularity rose to the great heights deplored by Friedländer. On Rumohr and Memling see above, note 31.

[41] Friedländer, *Die altniederländische Malerei* VI, pp. 54 f.

[42] Panofsky, *Early Netherlandish Painting*, p. 347.

[43] Friedländer, *Die altniederländische Malerei* VI, p. 56.

may prefer dynamic excess, but that does not justify my dismissing every example of classical balance as insipid and of minor value. Those artists whose temperaments seem calm are not necessarily inferior to the bold 'explorers' and 'inventors' whose discoveries they absorb. The belief that they are, and the very language of pioneering in which that belief is commonly expressed, are both products of what might be called the Agonistic Ascendancy in art-criticism. Was it perhaps because of his relentless energy as an 'inventor' that Roger, faced with the conventional task of representing the *Annunciation* as a marble group feigned in *grisaille* (fig. 110), should have carried the imitation of carving to such lengths as to picture all those ungainly props by which a sculptor would have had to support the more fragile parts of the carving? The lily, buttressed by five such pegs, has acquired a particularly home-made look, unless the prize belongs to the marble-dove, pinned to a marble-cloud on the wall. In defence of this eccentric performance it has been claimed that Roger was inspired by the *paragone* and meant to expose the shortcomings of sculpture,[44] but such a parodistic aim would be so little in keeping with the devotional solemnity of the Beaune altarpiece, and also so contrary to the respect that Roger habitually shows for the sculptor's craft in his paintings, that this freakish refinement is perhaps better explained as just another of Roger's studied archaisms. The laboured effect is worth comparing with the same subject in a *grisaille* by Memling where the marble-dove seems to fly without effort and without inviting our disbelief (fig. 111).[45]

It can be agreed that Memling was no pioneer. His art is harmonious, candid and serene; and so, one would suppose, was his Christianity. His altarpieces are not so much devoid of religious intensity as of Teutonic vehemence and apocalyptic vision;[46] they were designed to move the pious believer to humility, fortitude and resignation rather than to arouse

[44] H. Beenken, *Rogier van der Weyden* (1951), p. 67.

[45] Memling followed the precedent set by Jan van Eyck in the *grisaille* shutters of the small Dresden altarpiece (no. 799). In the – almost equally small – *grisaille* Annunciation of the Thyssen Collection (no. 133) Van Eyck used the optical device of setting the sculptures tight against a surface of dark polished stone which mirrors them – an artifice that mitigates the 'improbability' of the flying dove by creating a subsidiary illusion; but the problem did not disturb him in the Dresden *grisaille*. Memling's undisturbed image is particularly

notable because of its size (nearly eight times the height of the Van Eyck in Dresden). As the Van Eyck *grisailles* are datable in the 1430's, and Roger's *grisaille* about 1450, Memling's version – dated 1491 – is almost pointedly *retardataire*.

[46] When he did have to paint an apocalyptic vision – St. John on the island of Patmos (fig. 33) – he rendered the threatening parts with sufficient force (fig. 32), but he kept them small in comparison with the Heavenly Vision, which he depicted with affectionate exactitude, as if he had inspected every detail. Note the glass floor

the sinful to horror and despair.[47] The small biblical scenes in miniature style, which so often enliven the landscapes in the background, are mostly of a mysterious stillness, and particularly touching by the lyrical felicity with which they admit supernatural events. A solitary angel on the banks of the Jordan (fig. 27), the sun setting over the Sea of Galilee while Peter tries to walk on the water (fig. 130), the deserted hills from which the disciples compellingly witness the Ascension (fig. 129), these have the authority of a poetic vision that draws from the observation of nature. The frequency of hermit-saints in Memling's pictures, even when they were not required by the donors' names – St. Anthony the Hermit, St. Giles, St. Maur, St. Christopher aided by the hermit's lamp, St. Mary of Egypt – suggests that the burghers and friars whom he served had a touch of quietism in their religion.[48] The fact that he entered with sympathy into that mood, and made it the effective mood of his paintings, is surely a poor reason for down-grading him as an artist.

As a narrator Memling is so absorbed in the event to be reported that he can convey even a spoken word. In the *Ecce homo* (fig. 72) some of the crowd calling 'Crucify, crucify' cross their hands to signify their meaning: an uncommon gesture of obvious intent, vulgar and macabre.[49] Few artists have managed, in the hubbub of the *Ecce homo,* to raise the figure of Christ above the pitiable, as Memling has done here; or to display the in-effectual Pilate as an official of some refinement. To achieve these intimate descriptive touches, in which the Bultync panel is particularly rich (figs. 71, 77–81), Memling needed a diminutive scale; and this may explain his repeated use of a panorama-like prospect sprawling with incident – what Sulpiz Boisserée called *eine gemalte Krippe, eine Welt im Kleinen.*[50]

in which the architecture and brocade of the celestial throne, as well as one of the apocalyptic beasts, are mirrored.

[47] Even the Danzig *Last Judgement*, when compared with its model in Beaune, has a touch of reassurance in St. Michael's operation of the scales (see above, page 20).

[48] The four saints so impressively assembled in the Lübeck altarpiece (figs. 112–15) were the chosen patrons of a small *sodalitas* devoted to meditation. The donor (fig. 120), although a Hanseatic business man, was a native of the Rhineland, like Memling (see Voll, *Memling*, p. 174). On affinities between spiritual movements in the Rhineland, Flanders and England during the fifteenth century, see Dom Gerard Sitwell, *Medieval Spiritual Writers* (1961), pp. 107–40. So strong was the faith in the intercession of hermit-saints that in the Moreel triptych, for example, St. Christopher carrying the Child occupies the place in the centre, where the worshipper would normally expect to see the Virgin presenting the Child for adoration (fig. 87).

[49] The gesture lost much of its force in an *Ecce Homo* of the Roger School, clearly by an epigone (see above, page 17 note 2).

[50] See Sulpiz Boisserée, as quoted above, note 13. It would be a mistake to assume that because the two panoramas reproduced in figs. 70 and 71 belong to the same genre of painting, they must also belong to the same period of Memling's development. While the date of the Bultync panel (fig. 71) is recorded as 1480 (see above, note 13), the picture in Turin (fig. 70), if we

In his portraits Memling achieved a secure balance between the extremes of earthiness and idealisation – what might be described as a mitigated realism. Although all his likenesses are polite, it is hard to believe that any of them were meant to flatter[51]; that, for example, of Martin van Nieuwenhove, that young burgher of 23, coarse-featured and greasy of skin, has every appearance of fidelity to its original (fig. 152). Group compositions with innumerable faces, a task that might have stultified a less imaginative artist, seem to have given Memling particular pleasure: witness his skill and amused alertness in picturing intimate collocations of children's heads, both in portraiture (figs. 91, 96-7) and in religious illustration (fig. 98). The cumulative effect of so many adolescent expressions, interconnected by family likeness, recalls Leonardo da Vinci's method of demonstrating physiognomic affinities by juxtaposition, except that Leonardo did not concentrate these easily disconcerting exercises on young faces. A trace of Leonardo may be detected also in the design and mood of Memling's portrait of Benedetto Portinari, rendering the meditative character of this young Italian with profound but unsentimental sympathy (fig. 150). As for the landscapes that form the backgrounds to so many of his portraits, glimpsed between marble columns or out of open windows, stretching away behind the shoulders of his sitters, they are peaceful, decorative, poetic, civilized; though they are often exquisite miniatures which delight the beholder, they never distract his attention from the human figures in

---

accept that it was donated by Tommaso and Maria Portinari (cf. above, note 21), must have been painted in 1470. This follows from the fact that the Portinaris were married in that year (Warburg, *op. cit.*, p. 197) and that their first child, Margherita, who is still absent from the picture, was born in 1471 (*ibid.*, p. 378). Compared with the 'open form' adopted for the donors' portraits in the Bultync panel (fig. 80 f.), the strict symmetry imposed on them in the Turin picture looks archaic (figs. 75 f.) and might easily be ten years earlier. Indeed, the dramatic density of the panorama of the *Passion* (figs. 70, 73) agrees well with a date close to the Danzig *Last Judgement* (inscribed 1467, as noted above, page 24), but would be difficult to reconcile with the diaphanous type of composition characteristic of Memling by 1478-80 (cf. figs. 71, 77 ff.). Also the parallelism between the kneeling Christ and the kneeling donor at either end of this picture (fig. 70) is a more literal device than Memling would have cared to use later.

[51] An unexpected example of Memling's wit is the lissom portrait of a young woman (fig. 137) with a carnation as symbol of betrothal (Metropolitan Museum of Art, New York; cf. H. B. Wehle and M. Salinger, *Catalogue of Early Flemish, Dutch and German Paintings*, 1947, pp. 64 f.). To judge by the setting, under an arch, behind a parapet and in front of a landscape, the image belongs unquestionably, as Friedländer observed (*Die altniederländische Malerei* VI, p. 119, nos. 16A-B, pl. XIX), to the same design as an emblematic painting (fig. 138) of two horses attended by a little monkey (Van Beuningen Collection, Boymans Museum, Rotterdam). To imagine these two pictures joined as a diptych is (*pace* Panofsky, *op. cit.*, pp. 506 f. note 7) intolerable. They clearly were parts of a polyptych, of which two panels are now missing: next to the bride belongs a bridegroom, to whom the flower is pointing and who would be attended by the emblematic animals that signify (as Panofsky explained) his amorous passion. Conversely, the stallions, if understood as the bridegroom's emblem, call for an answering attribute on the side of the bride: presumably (in the best Petrarchan fashion) a pair of unicorns controlled by a cupid. Since

the foreground.[52] Here, as in the allegorical flowerpieces that appear as attributes of the Virgin,[53] Memling's sweetness avoids the mawkish by what may seem the merest hair's-breadth, but it does avoid it.

Why then have art-historians turned against him? Largely, I think, because he came at the end of one tradition, not at the beginning of another. He founded no school; his pupils and followers were of negligible interest and the masters of the next generation owed little to him; historically speaking his art is a terminus, not even the starting-point of a branch line. With historians that is nearly enough to damn him: he was not a 'progressive'; and those scholars who devote themselves to the study of early Netherlandish painting, believe in progress. That is their great un-examined premise – or it may be only one of several.

Indeed there are signs here that progress may mean two rather different things. The simpler, more obvious meaning would limit the term to the growth of technical mastery: the better understanding and application of the laws of linear and aerial perspective, of light and shadow, of colour modulation, of human anatomy, physiognomics, and so forth. It would be foolish to deny that in this sense there was progress in the Low Countries during the course of the fifteenth century, that in painting as in music men could there and then have spoken (but did not) of an *ars nova* or a *nouvelle pratique*.[54] Nor can there be any valid objection to the use of such evidences

the group of horses is derived from a detail in the Bultync panel (fig. 79), the date of this little set is after 1480, and perhaps the emblematic part is primarily a workshop product. Apart from the *Man with a Coin of Nero* (fig. 141), this is the only emblematic portrait ascribed to Memling, and one wonders whether it too was perhaps an Italian commission.

[52] I am aware of Friedländer's opinion (*Landscape – Portrait – Still Life*, 1949, p. 38) that in Memling's portraits 'attention is drawn away from the individual personality and is dissipated over the countryside'; I can only say that mine is not.

[53] The most provocative of these allegorical still-lifes is the one in the Thyssen Collection (fig. 145), which is painted on the back of the handsome portrait of a man in prayer (fig. 144). Filled with flowers sacred to the Virgin (lilies, irises and columbine), the majolica jug with the sacred monogram (which should read *yhs*) is virtually the same as in a painting of the Virgin and Child in Berlin, also ascribed to Memling (fig. 146). As may be seen from specimens illustrated by B. Rackham (*Italian Maiolica*, 1952, p. 14, pls. 16 and 27b; also his *Catalogue of Italian Maiolica, Victoria and Albert Museum*,

1940, frontispiece = no. 128A; pl. 26 = no. 147; pl. 33 = no. 123), the sacred monogram in a flaming circle, known as the badge of San Bernardino da Siena, was fairly common on Italian pottery of the fifteenth century. If the jug in the Thyssen picture is Italian, this may also be the nationality of the sitter; his features would not speak against it (fig. 144). However, as both sides of this panel have been boldly refurbished, the authenticity of details is very uncertain. The faulty design of the mono-gram, and a coarse error of perspective in the geometric ornament below the lid, show insecurities of handling in just those parts on which the picture in Berlin does not give any guidance (compare fig. 146). To draw any further conclusions would be improper without a thorough examination of the evidence, both physical and documentary. The Thyssen Catalogue (*Sammlung Schloss Rohoncz*, 1958, p. 72, no. 281a) is unhelpful.

[54] On this see Panofsky, *op. cit.* I, pp. 150 f. Except for some visibly musical angels (figs. 4, 108), we have no information of any kind concerning Memling's know-ledge of music. It would have been pleasant to include among his patrons so remarkable a personage as Giles Joye, parish-priest of the *Oude Kerk* in Delft, prebendary

of progress as a means of dating or of pinpointing one artist's indebtedness to others. When so many pictures are undocumented any help is likely to be of value. But technical progress, however widely it be defined, is by itself a fallible guide to even historical importance. If, for example, it is said that the panels of Jacques Daret 'are distinctly progressive, being no less advanced in craftsmanship than the works of even his greatest contemporaries', it is not intended that they should bulk at all large in the history of Franco-Flemish painting.[55]

But 'progressive' on the lips of art-historians seems often to mean something which has little directly to do with technical advance, is much less definite and therefore all the more emotive. A painter may be described as progressive because he seems to have gone further along the road which his art was destined to follow, or which the historian perhaps thinks it ought to have followed. Movement along the highway is best, but it is better to be carried down a byway than not to move at all.[56] Art does not stand still even for a moment of perfection. Because history is concerned with movement, the degree to which an artist is responsible for change is the measure of his significance. To fall behind is to invite condemnation and dismissal as 'retarded' and 'reactionary', though escape is possible if it can be said that 'he remained, like many revolutionaries, deeply committed to the past.'[57] Each newcomer is to be judged by the strenuousness with which he holds his own; for example: 'being Roger's junior by some ten years, Petrus Christus had to come to terms with one who had already welded the styles of the founders [i.e. Jan van Eyck and the Master of Flémalle] into a formidable unity. He had to achieve a second synthesis, so to speak, and this was possible only by a partial cancellation of the first. . . . His is one of the cases, by no means rare in the history of art, in which gains were possible only with the loss of values already acquired, a case of progress through renunciation.'[58] Similarly Roger van der Weyden

---

of St. Donatian at Bruges, one time chaplain to Philip the Good and Charles the Bold, a leading musician in the ducal *capella domestica* and a composer of some renown: he has been convincingly identified as the subject of a portrait dated 1472, now at the Clark Art Institute, Williamstown, Mass., but the attribution of this painting to Memling (Friedländer, *Die altniederländische Malerei* VI, p. 129 no. 72, pl. XL) is not as conclusive as the iconographic demonstration (F. van Molle, *Identification d'un portrait de Gilles Joye attribué à Memling*, 1960).

[55] Panofsky, *op. cit. T*, p. 158. Equally telling is the fact that Petrus Christus, of whom Friedländer observes that 'his dependence on Jan van Eyck amounts almost to parasitism' (*Von Eyck bis Bruegel*, p. 20), employed a system of linear perspective more 'advanced' scientifically than that of his host.

[56] The metaphor will be found in Friedländer, *ibid.*, p. 62.

[57] Panofsky, *op. cit.* I, pp. 164 and 350.

[58] *ibid.*, pp. 308–10.

'arrived at his apparently archaic solutions not only from an entirely "modern" starting point but also for a very "modern" purpose: . . . he attempted to break new ground by the old device of *reculer pour mieux sauter*'.[59] It is some slight consolation to discover in another instance that while 'progress was possible only on one of two roads' these were at least roads 'leading in opposite directions';[60] and one is left suspecting that the reason why these alone were 'possible' was because they were in fact both taken and, what is more, ultimately converged. This whole-hearted reliance upon what to others may seem a coarse identification of 'progress' with 'innovation', and preferably dramatic innovation, allows Memling's claims upon our attention to be quickly disposed of. He was retarded when he should have been advancing; he ought more obviously to have gone one better than his predecessors. His 'pleasant exploitation of inherited wealth' was no substitute for 'courage and enterprise'.[61] As a prosperous burgher of Bruges who gave his customers what they evidently wanted, he would have understood the entrepreneurial metaphor without necessarily admitting its justice to his own case. It is left to us to wonder whether the history of art really bears much resemblance to the management of an old-established family business. But even if it does there is still no justification for regarding courage and enterprise as necessarily and always superior to prudence and circumspection; or more deserving of the historian's interest. To equate novelty with life is to adopt a needlessly philistine solution to every historian's inescapable problem: how to distinguish the significant from the trivial. No mere rule of thumb can relieve him from the need to exercise his own judgement and consider pictures, like other historical 'facts', on their merits. For the historian Memling's at least possess the initial advantage of having been highly prized in his own day. Even if his patrons' taste may seem to us questionable, it is not something that can be left entirely out of the reckoning.

Least of all may it be ignored by the historian who wishes to understand the religious outlook of an influential section of Western European society not long before the Reformation. Memling's great popularity with the educated laity of the second half of the fifteenth century, even if he appealed more to the merchant than to the courtier, means that his works reflected,

59 *ibid.*, p. 250.
   ibid., p. 289.

61 Friedländer, *Von Eyck bis Bruegel*, p. 84.

and may have helped to form, the mind of his age and class. We have been told to associate the waning of the Middle Ages with an hysterical fear of the Day of Judgement, a morbid preoccupation with such themes as the Dance of Death and the eternal pains of hell, a fascinated and realistically expressed disgust with the corruptions of the world of the flesh.[62] It would be difficult to argue that Memling was out of tune with his times. Yet there is hardly a trace of such morbidity in his work. The not infrequent occasions on which he had to paint a Crucifixion or the martyrdom of a saint (figs. 26, 74, 107, 116–19, 121 f., 131) provide little evidence of a fondness for the charnel-house side of late-medieval Christianity;[63] it was not a vein he was tempted to exploit.[64] He was the artist of passive resignation and the larger hope. And as such he was so much in demand as a painter that he became one of the more well-to-do citizens of opulent Bruges. Evidently the *Totentanz* can be allowed to bulk too large in our reconstruction of the beliefs of that time. If one of the most widely-admired artists of the last third of the fifteenth century preferred hope to fear, the usurers and money-changers may not after all have been quite so haunted by the prospect of hell-fire as it is the fashion to believe. Doubtless some were. But if they wanted a painter to make their flesh creep they did not employ Memling.

[62] See J. Huizinga, *The Waning of the Middle Ages* (1924), *passim*.

[63] If in the *Martyrdom of St. Sebastian* the triumphant posture silences the pain (fig. 131), the impassibility of *St. Giles*, whose arm was pierced by the arrow from which he saved the deer (figs. 89, 115), does not suggest any wound at all. Even the face of Christ is seen unhurt in *Veronica's Napkin* (fig. 132), without the marks from the crown of thorns that are generally part of this image.

[64] It is noteworthy that in so comprehensive a collection of sacred histories as are assembled in the Bultync panorama (fig. 71), the sufferings of Christ do not appear.

To see all the events that followed after the Passion – the Resurrection, the *Noli me tangere*, the Journey to Emmaus, Christ calling Peter over the Sea of Galilee, Christ appearing to his Mother, the Ascension, the Pentecost – without any image of the Passion itself is indeed uncommon, but justified by a programme concentrated on epiphanies (see above, page 30). The picture may have served as a sort of predella to a large fourteenth-century *Crucifixion* that was probably the main altarpiece of the Tanners' chapel, now in the Cathedral Museum at Bruges; see L. van Puyvelde, *La peinture flamande au siècle des Van Eyck*, p. 55: 'Le Calvaire des Tanneurs'.

Appendices

APPENDIX 1

*A List of Documented Dates related to Memling and his Works**

1464   Death of Roger van der Weyden, to whom Memling was apprenticed in Brussels (see Vasari, *Vite di alcuni Fiamminghi*).

1465   Registration of Memling as a citizen of Bruges, native of Seligenstadt.

1467   Date inscribed on the Danzig *Last Judgement*.

1470   Marriage of Tommaso Portinari and Maria Baroncelli, portrayed by Memling as a young pair (Metropolitan Museum of Art, New York).

1472   Date inscribed on the Ottawa *Virgin and Child, with Donor and St. Anthony Abbot* (formerly Liechtenstein Collection).

1475   Death of Antonis Seghers, portrayed as a donor on one of the shutters of the *Mystic Marriage of St. Catherine*, completed 1479 (see below).

1478   Presentation to the Stationers' Guild at Bruges of a panel of the *Passion* commissioned from Memling by Willem Vrelant. The Guild commissions shutters for this panel, again to be supplied by Memling. Completed 1480 (see below).

1479   Triptych, *Adoration of the Magi*, donated to St. John's Hospital in Bruges by Jan Floreins, aged 36, as inscribed on the painting, which agrees with the date 1479 on the frame.

1479   Completion of the *Mystic Marriage of St. Catherine* (dated on frame) for the high altar of St. John's Hospital, Bruges; commissioned at least four years earlier (see 1475).

1480   Completion and installation in the Guild chapel of the work first presented to the Stationers' Guild in Bruges by Willem Vrelant in 1478 (see above).

1480   Presentation to the Tanners' Guild, by Pieter Bultync and his wife Katelyne, of a panel by Memling representing the *Adoration of the Magi* and other epiphanies (now Alte Pinakothek, Munich).

1480   Date inscribed on the frame of a triptych, *The Lamentation*, donated by Adriaen Reyns to St. John's Hospital, Bruges.

---

*While no contemporary documents have been found that refer to Memling before he became a citizen in Bruges (1465), for the last thirty years of his life (1465–94) the documentation is not only abundant, but perhaps more complete in the dating of works than for any other master of the fifteenth century. Although some of the frames carrying inscriptions and dates are no longer in their original condition, the dates they record are of documentary value, even if retraced: see above page 4 note 23; also page 13 note 61.

1480 Memling registers an apprentice with the Corporation of Painters in Bruges. As Memling is listed here as 'Meester Jan van Memmelynghe',* it is clear that he was a master of the guild, even though the record of his admission appears to be lost.

1482 *Annunciation* (Collection Robert Lehman, New York), dated on original frame, now replaced.

1483 Memling registers another apprentice.*

1484 Triptych, with *St. Maur, St. Christopher and St. Giles*, donated by Willem Moreel and his wife Barbara to the family chapel at the church of St. James in Bruges (now Municipal Museum, Bruges).

1487 Date inscribed on the *Portrait of Benedetto Portinari* (Uffizi, Florence).

1487 Diptych with *Portrait of Martin van Nieuwenhove*, aged 23, dated on frame (St. John's Hospital, Bruges).

1487 Death of Memling's wife, *née* Anne de Valkenaere, whom he had married between 1470 and 1480.

1489 Consecration of the *Shrine of St. Ursula* (St. John's Hospital, Bruges).

1489–90 Plague, preceding the completion of the Jacob Floreins Altarpiece (now Louvre, Paris).

1491 Lübeck Altarpiece, dated on frame.

1494 Death of Memling.

1495 Memling's three sons still under age (guardian's report).

* C. Vanden Haute, *La Corporation des Peintres de Bruges* (Bruges n.d.), p. 28, also p. 35.

APPENDIX 2

A List of Memling's known Patrons[*]

Pieter Bultync, member of the Tanners' Guild, Bruges

Agnes Casembrood, sister at St. John's Hospital, Bruges

Sir John Donne of Kidwelly, in the service of Edward IV at Calais

Josina van Dudzeele, sister at St. John's Hospital, Bruges

Jacob Floreins, member of the Corporation of Merchant Grocers, Bruges

Jan Floreins, friar at St. John's Hospital, Bruges, temporarily master

Heinrich Greverade, banker and merchant in Lübeck

Clara van Hulsen, sister at St. John's Hospital, Bruges

Jacob de Kueninc, friar at St. John's Hospital, Bruges

Anna van den Moortele, sister at St. John's Hospital, Bruges

Willem Moreel, member of the Corporation of Merchant Grocers, twice burgomaster of Bruges

Martin van Nieuwenhove, merchant-patrician, later town-councillor and burgomaster of Bruges

Benedetto Portinari, junior partner of the Portinari firm in Bruges after its separation from the Medici bank

Tommaso Portinari, factor of the Medici bank in Bruges, 1465–1480

Adriaen Reyns, friar at St. John's Hospital, Bruges

Antonis Seghers, friar at St. John's Hospital, Bruges

Angelo Tani, factor of the Medici bank in Bruges, 1455–1464

Willem Vrelant, miniaturist and founding member of the Stationers' Guild, Bruges

[*] Persons whose patronage of Memling has been inferred from inconclusive heraldic evidence (Jean du Celier, Francisco de Royas), or from a conjectural attribution (Giles Joye), or from portraits that survive only in copies (Anthony of Burgundy, James of Savoy), have been omitted from this list. We have, however, included the donor of the Danzig *Last Judgement*, Angelo Tani, on the assumption that Memling had a hand in it. On all the persons named see Index, s.v.

APPENDIX 3

Memorandum on the Date of the Donne Triptych

§1. The transfer of Sir John Donne's death from 1469 to 1503[1] removes the only substantial reason for wishing to date the triptych painted for him by Hans Memling among that artist's earliest known works. If Donne (like his brother Henry) had been among the Welsh gentlemen who fell at Edgecote on 26 July 1469 and if the daughter who appears at her mother's side in the triptych was the only one of their four known children to have been born before it was commissioned, it inevitably followed that the picture could not have been begun much later than 1467. Even this left so little room for the births of two (let alone three) more children that G. Hulin de Loo found it wise to imagine that Memling might have paid an unrecorded visit to England in 1466. The discovery that Donne, who was not knighted until 1471, in fact outlived Memling himself has the result of detaching the triptych from its chronological moorings to drift at large within the wide limits of Edward IV's reign. For the livery collars worn by the Donnes make it certain that their portraits were not painted before 1461 and at least improbable that they were painted after Richard III's usurpation, still more Henry VII's. The question is whether any evidence exists which makes it possible to assign a more definite date within the span of these twenty-two years.

§2. As a portrait-painter Memling did not perhaps indulge in flattery, but he was on the whole kind. In the Donne triptych he has not concealed the fact that the wrinkles and thinning hair of Sir John Donne contrast strongly with the youthful beauty of his wife. If Memling portrayed his patron at an age of, say, fifty, this would date the altarpiece about 1480: for John Donne, the youngest son of Griffith Donne, was born not later than 1430. We have no comparable certainty for the year in which Elizabeth Hastings was born; but her marriage to Donne in (or slightly before) 1465 was nearly twelve years later than that of her sister Joan and some seventeen later than that of her sister Anne. It is therefore probable that she was born at the tail-end of Sir Leonard Hastings' large family. The date of her maternal grandmother's birth (12 February 1371) does not rule out the possibility that Elizabeth Hastings was born about 1450, that she was her husband's junior by some twenty years. If he married her in or shortly before 1465 (when she is first mentioned as his wife in the re-granting of royal favours),

[1] In so far as this Memorandum, originally compiled for the National Gallery, rests on documents already quoted in Part I, pages 2 ff. notes 11–52, the references will not be repeated here. Only a few additions are given in the notes that follow.

it would follow that neither in 1466 nor in 1468 could they have had a child of the age that is shown in the painting. On that evidence alone the picture would have to be dated several years later.

§3. In view of the strong evidence supporting Panofsky's claim that the omission 'even of babes in arms' from a devotional painting of this kind 'would have amounted to a *diminutio capitis*' (see above, page 3 note 17), it would be foolish to maintain, without further reasons, that the Donne triptych is a rare breach of what was certainly a general rule. We must therefore accept the probability that when the picture was painted the Donnes had only the one child that is represented in it. If it could be determined when that child was born, and what were the birth-dates of any brothers or sisters, this would be an important step toward settling the date of the painting.

§4. Little is known about Anne Donne, the eldest of the Donne children who survived infancy. She was in her thirties when she died. Her husband, Sir William Rede of Boarstall, succeeded his grandfather in 1489 at the age of twenty-two; that is, he was born about, almost certainly in, 1467; and he lived until 1526–7. By 1510, if not before, he had married another Anne, niece of Archbishop Warham, by whom he had two daughters. The first Anne's daughters, Elizabeth and Mary Rede, are mentioned in Lady Donne's will, but she herself is not: which suggests that she had died before 29 November 1507. Her son Leonard (presumably named after his mother's maternal grandfather Sir Leonard Hastings) was almost certainly of age by 1521. Since Anne's marriage to William Rede was arranged by their families it may have occurred as early as her fifteenth year; her husband may or may not have been older. Her birth as early as 1467 (which was the year of her husband's birth) is possible, but 1470–1 is the more likely date and it may well have been a year or two later.

§5. Three further children of the Donnes who survived infancy, two boys and a girl, are recorded:

(*a*) The eldest son, Sir Edward Donne (knighted in 1513), was alive on 24 December 1551 when he made an addition to his will. He died near the beginning of 1552. The approximate date of his birth (after January 1482 but not later than November 1486) may be inferred from the fact that he was not yet of age on 23 January 1503, when his father's will left both lands and goods to his widow; but that on 29 November 1507 his mother's will made him her sole executor and residuary legatee. He is first heard of as one of the gentlemen-ushers of the king's chamber on 3 July 1503 when he was granted the succession to his father's office as keeper of the park of Risborough, Bucks.[2] The earliest references to his marriage (to Anne daughter of Sir John Verney of Middle Claydon, Bucks) are found in a letter to him from his brother written shortly before 6 January 1509,[3] and in his mother-in-law's will drawn up on 3 April 1509.[4] The absence of any reference to his wife in his mother's will, although it contains mention of a good

---

[2] *Cal. Pat. Rolls, 1494–1509*, p. 319.
[3] Newton Dunn, *Genealogies of the Dwnns*, pp. 17 f.

[4] *Letters and Papers of the Verney Family*, ed. J. Bruce (Camden Society 1863), pp. 39 ff.

many members of the Donne family and its connections, is some slight indication that the marriage took place some time after November 1507. Edward's active career did not really begin until the accession of Henry VIII, and there is nothing in the record of his public life to require his birth before 1483. Presumably he was named after his father's generous master.

(b) There is no need to waste time over Sir Griffith Donne since he was obviously Sir Edward's junior. It should however be emphasised that nothing is known about Sir Griffith's career to make it necessary to suppose that he was born before 1487. His request to his older brother in December 1508 or January 1509 to be given the legacy left him by their mother and his promise to be ordered by Edward's pleasure make it likely that he was only just of age;[5] and he was made to wait until 24 December 1509.[6] As one of Henry VIII's chosen companions in the many physical exploits that marked that prince's adolescence and young manhood (Henry was born in 1491), Griffith Donne was the contemporary of such men as Charles Brandon (c.1484–1545), in whose household he later resided, and Giles Capel (b. 1485).[7] He remained a knight of the king's body for most of his life, and was clearly a distinguished horseman.[8] Unlike his father and his elder brother, who were by contemporary knightly standards exceptionally long-lived, he died under sixty, in 1543.[9]

(c) Margaret Donne married her father's ward (bought by him from the executors of William Lord Hastings), Edward Trussell, heir to an estate of more than £350 p.a. Her husband was born in 1478, probably in the second half of that year since he was thought to be still under age in the spring of 1499 when he died leaving a son, John, aged

---

[5] Newton Dunn, loc. cit.

[6] Bodleian MS Douce 393, fol. 1.

[7] On Griffith Donne's participation in Henry VIII's Coronation Tournament and in the Westminster Tournament of 1511 see The Great Tournament Roll of Westminster, ed. S. Anglo (1968), p. 46 note 1, pp. 111, 114.

[8] It was in that capacity that he travelled on Henry VIII's behalf in Italy: on 30 October 1514 Giuliano de' Medici thanked Henry VIII for the gift of two caparisoned horses presented to him by Sir Griffith Donne (Rymer, Foedera XIII, p. 467; Letters and Papers . . . of Henry VIII, I, second edition, no. 3395). A few weeks later, 21 November 1514, Francesco Gonzaga, having received a royal present by Sir Griffith Donne and learned from him that the king is fond of horses, sends Henry VIII twelve brood mares from his celebrated Mantuan stables (ibid., no. 3459). For negotiations about horses with Alfonso d'Este in Ferrara, who had received 'two caparisoned palfreys and a horn' from Sir Griffith Donne, see Letters and Papers III, i, no. 479. In a letter from Calais, dated 28 January 1518 (Letters and Papers II, no. 3906), Sir John Wilsher reports to Henry VIII that Sir Griffith Donne has arrived 'with the goodliest sort of mares of the realm of Naples and other of Turkey, such as I have

never seen in these parts, so as your grace shall be within a short while out of danger of any prince for coursers of Naples'. A payment of 1000 mks 'for Sir Griffith Donne, over sea' (Letters and Papers II, p. 1465) may have some bearing on this sort of transaction.

[9] Griffith Donne's will, dated 2 October 1542 (Prerogative Court of Canterbury, 7 Pynnyng), was proved London 19 May 1544. In 1543, Delamers manor in Wheathampstead, which he held from his wife for life, passed to his step-daughter Grissel, wife of Sir John Boteler (Victoria County History: Hertfordshire II, 1908, p. 299). Griffith Donne's daughter Elizabeth, his only child, was very young when he died: his will placed her under the guidance of Dr. John Hughes, whose son Thomas she later married. It is not impossible that she was born after the death of her cousin, Elizabeth Donne, the daughter of Edward, again an only child, who predeceased her father, as shown in his will (P.C.C., F. 1 Powell). Since Griffith's daughter appears to have been the last surviving member of the family to have borne the name of Donne, and of Elizabeth Donne (see Genealogical Table, page 57), it was probably through her that the Donne altarpiece passed by direct descent to the Duke of Devonshire (see National Gallery Catalogue, ed. cit., pp. 126 f.).

between one and two years, and a daughter, Elizabeth, born in 1496 (afterwards Countess of Oxford). After Edward Trussell's death his widow married Thomas Cardigan. She is mentioned in her mother's will, none too cordially.[10] If we are right in assuming that her sister Anne would not have been born earlier than her husband (1467), the same would apply also to Margaret (1478): the most likely date of her birth, considering that of her children, would be 1480–1.

§6. The evidence, however circumstantial, that Margaret Donne was born c1480–1, Edward Donne c1483 and Griffith Donne c1487, seems to indicate that Anne Donne was considerably the senior of the Donne's four surviving children. She may in fact have been as much as eleven years older than the eldest of the others. It was therefore not impossible for the Donnes to have been painted as late as 1480 in the company of a single child.

§7. If one approaches Memling's dated or reasonably datable works in search of those that can most convincingly be associated with the Donne triptych, that which possesses the most obvious affinities with it is the great altarpiece painted for the Hospital of St. John at Bruges and dated 1479 on the frame. There can be little doubt that but for the false scent provided by Sir John's supposed death in 1469 the Donne triptych would have been assigned to about the same date, that is to say to the late 1470's. There is nothing in the circumstances of Sir John Donne's life nor in the ages of his children to render such a date improbable, and very much to make the date 1466–8 impossible.

§8. The late 1470's, to which the painting should be ascribed on stylistic grounds, were years of growing prosperity for the Donnes, and 1480 saw their acquisition of the manors of Horsenden, Saunderton and Druels in Bledlow which established the family in Buckinghamshire and for the first time definitely in England[11] (their earlier enjoyment of the Tresham estates in various counties by Edward IV's grant had been of brief duration). The rich knightly landowner of 1480 was undoubtedly a much more likely patron than the rising esquire of the royal household could have been in the 1460's.

§9. In conclusion it should perhaps be said that the much discussed problem of finding a particular date on which Donne and his family could have visited Bruges does in fact not exist. Apart from an embassy to the French court in February and March 1477 he could easily have gone to Bruges at any time between 1470 and Edward IV's death. For it was not until 1484–5 that he filled the office of sheriff in Buckinghamshire and was obliged to be resident in his bailiwick.[12] Before that date various offices he held under Edward IV obliged him to reside at Calais, not much more than sixty miles from Bruges and thus within easy reach of Memling's studio.

[10] P.C.C. 32 Adeane: 'upon her good obeying to me and mine executor'.

[11] *Victoria County History, Buckinghamshire* II (1908),

pp. 248, 254; III (1925), p. 93.

[12] *Cal. Pat. Rolls, 1476–84*, p. 488.

APPENDIX 4
*Genealogical Table of Sir John Donne's Family**

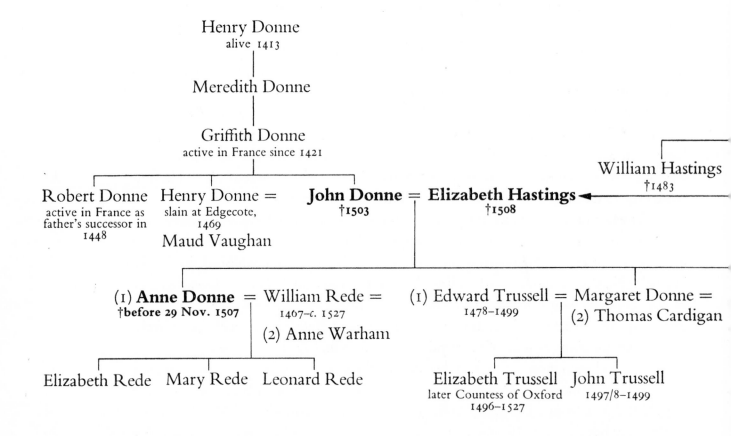

* The three names printed in bold face refer to the persons portrayed in Memling's altarpiece (fig. 1). To show that Elizabeth Hastings was probably Sir Leonard Hastings's youngest child, her brothers and sisters are also listed. Otherwise the Table is confined to names actually mentioned in the text. A more complete genealogy of the Donnes, the Hastings and the Redes would have to include much guesswork and marginal information that does not bear directly on the present subject. On variant spellings of the name Donne see above, page 2 note 11.

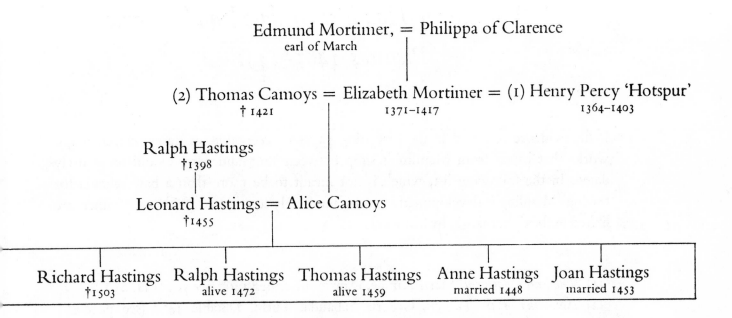

Edmund Mortimer, = Philippa of Clarence
earl of March

(2) Thomas Camoys = Elizabeth Mortimer = (1) Henry Percy 'Hotspur'
†1421   1371–1417   1364–1403

Ralph Hastings
†1398

Leonard Hastings = Alice Camoys
†1455

Richard Hastings   Ralph Hastings   Thomas Hastings   Anne Hastings   Joan Hastings
†1503   alive 1472   alive 1459   married 1448   married 1453

Edward Donne = Anne Verney   Griffith Donne = Elizabeth Roche-Eden
†1552   †1543   †1541

Grissel Roche = John Boteler

Thomas Jones = Elizabeth Donne   Thomas Hughes = Elizabeth Donne
†1559   †before 1551   †1587   unmarried 1542
                                                  †1590

(1) Edward Neville, = Grissel Hughes = (2) Francis Clifford,
lord Bergavenny   †1613   earl of Cumberland
†1589   †1641

Cliffords
Boyles
Cavendishes

APPENDIX 5

A Provisional Handlist of dated and datable Pictures 1467–1491

If the evidence collected in the foregoing pages is acceptable, at least nineteen major works that issued from Memling's shop between 1467 and 1491 would be securely dated. In the following list, which is not meant to be more than a bare schema for tracing Memling's development, works intimately connected with each other are linked in the right margin by a bracket.

(1) *The Last Judgement,* Marienkirche, Danzig. Inscribed 1467 (see pages 24, 25 f.)

(2) *Panorama of the Passion,* Galleria Sabauda, Turin. Datable 1470 (see page 41 note 50)

(3) *Portraits of Tommaso and Maria Portinari,* Metropolitan Museum of Art, New York. Closely related in date and lay-out to the donors' portraits in no. (2), possibly painted from the same maquettes

(4) *Virgin and Child, with Donor and St. Anthony Abbot,* National Gallery of Canada, Ottawa. Inscribed 1472 (see page 13 note 61)

(5) *St. John's Altarpiece* ('Mystic Marriage of St. Catherine'), St. John's Hospital, Bruges. Commissioned in or before 1475, completed 1479 (see page 34 note 25)

(6) *The Donne Triptych,* National Gallery, London. Closely related in date and plan to no. (5); *c*1479–80 (=donor's age *c*50)

(7) *The Jan Floreins Triptych* ('The Adoration of the Magi'), St. John's Hospital, Bruges. Donor's age inscribed 36 (=1479 on frame)

(8) *Panorama of Epiphanies* (centred in 'The Adoration of the Magi'), Alte Pinakothek, Munich. Donated by Pieter Bultync 1480

(9) *The Adoration of the Magi,* Prado, Madrid. Largely workshop product, based on (7) and (8), on an expanded scale; *c*1480

(10) *The Reyns Triptych* ('The Lamentation'), St. John's Hospital, Bruges. Inscribed on frame 1480

(11) *The Annunciation,* Collection Robert Lehman, New York. Originally dated on frame, 1482

(12) *The Moreel Triptych,* Musée Communal des Beaux-Arts, Bruges. Donated 1484 ⎤

(13) *Portraits of Willem and Barbara Moreel,* Musée Royal des Beaux-Arts, Brussels. ⎬
Closely related in date and lay-out to the donors' portraits in no. (12). ⎦

(14) *Portrait of Benedetto Portinari,* Uffizi, Florence. Inscribed 1487 ⎤
⎬
(15) *Half-length of St. Benedict,* Uffizi, Florence. Companion piece to no. (14) ⎦

(16) *Diptych of Martin van Nieuwenhove,* St. John's Hospital, Bruges. Inscribed on frame
1487, with donor's age as 23

(17) *Shrine of St. Ursula,* St. John's Hospital, Bruges. Consecrated 1489

(18) *The Jacob Floreins Altarpiece,* Louvre, Paris. Completed after the plague of 1489–90

(19) *The Heinrich Greverade Altarpiece* ('The Passion'), Domkirche, Lübeck. Inscribed on
the frame 1491

Bibliography

ANGLO, S., ed., *The Great Tournament Roll of Westminster* (1968)

ARU, C., *see* 'Corpus des primitifs flamands'

BALDASS, L. von, *Hans Memling* (1942)

BEENKEN, H., *Rogier van der Weyden* (1951)

BIALOSTOCKI, J., *see* 'Corpus des primitifs flamands'

BISTHOVEN, A. J. de, *see* 'Corpus des primitifs flamands'

BOCK, Franz, *Memling-Studien* (1900)

BOISSERÉE, Mathilde, ed., *Sulpiz Boisserée* (1862)

BREWER, J. S., *see* London, Public Record Office

BROCKWELL, M. W., 'A Danzig Altarpiece attributed to Memling', *The Connoisseur* CIV (1939), pp. 258 f.

'A Document concerning Memling', *The Connoisseur* CIV (1939), pp. 186 f.

BRUCE, J., *Letters and Papers of the Verney Family* (1853)

CARR, A. D., 'Welshmen and the Hundred Years' War', *The Welsh History Review* IV (1968), pp. 21–46

CONWAY, M. W., *The Van Eycks and their Followers* (1921)

COREMANS, P., with R. SNEYERS and J. THISSEN, 'Memlinc's Mystiek Hulwelijk van de H. Katharina, Onderzoek en Behandeling', *Bulletin de l'Institut Royal du Patrimoine Artistique* II (1959), pp. 83–96

Corpus des primitifs flamands:

ARU, C., and E. de GERADON, *La Galerie Sabauda de Turin* (1952)

BIALOSTOCKI, J., *Les musées de Pologne* (1966)

BISTHOVEN, A. J. de, *Musée Communal des Beaux-Arts, Bruges* (1959)

LAVALLEYE, J., *Collections d'Espagne* (1953–8)

CROWE, J. A., and G. B. CAVALCASELLE, *The Early Flemish Painters* (1857)

DAVIES, Martin, *National Gallery Catalogue: Early Netherlandish School* (1968)

DELAISSÉ, L. M. J., *A Century of Dutch Manuscript Illumination* (1968)

La miniature flamande, le mécénat de Philippe le Bon, Exhibition (Brussels 1959)

DELAPIERRE, C., and A. VOISIN, *La Châsse de Sainte Ursule* (1841)

DESCAMPS, J. B., *La vie des peintres flamands* (1753)

DOPPERE, Romboudt de, *see* Dussart

DROST, W., *Das Jüngste Gericht des Hans Memling in der Marienkirche zu Danzig* (1941)

DUNN, T. W. Newton, *The Genealogies of the Dwnns of South Wales* (1953)

DURRIEU, Paul, *La miniature flamande au temps de la la cour de Bourgogne* (1927)

DUSSART, H., *Fragments inédits de Romboudt de Doppere: chronique brugeoise de 1491 à 1498* (1892)

Dwnn, Lewys, *Heraldic Visitations of Wales*, ed. S. R. Meyrick (1846)

Ellis, Henry, *Original Letters illustrative of English History* I (1827)

Fierens-Gevaert, *Histoire de la peinture flamande* (1927–9)

Fiorillo, J. D., *Geschichte der zeichnenden Künste in Deutschland und den vereinigten Niederlanden* (1817)

Flanders in the Fifteenth Century, Exhibition Catalogue (Detroit 1960)

Florence, Archivio di Stato, *Carteggio Mediceo avanti il Principato, filza 84, carta 32 bis, ter*

Förster, Ernst, *Denkmale deutscher Kunst* IX, iii (1864): 'Das Danziger Bild'

Friedländer, Max J., *Die altniederländische Malerei* II (1924), VI (1928), XIV (1937)
  Landscape – Portrait – Still Life (1949)
  'Noch etwas über das Verhältnis Roger van der Weydens zu Memling', *Oud Holland* LXI (1946), pp. 11–19
  'The Memling Exhibition at Bruges', *The Burlington Magazine* LXXV (1939), pp. 123 f.
  Von Eyck bis Bruegel (1916)

Fromentin, Eugène, *Les maîtres d'autrefois* (1876)

Frondeville, H. de, *La Vicomté d'Orbec pendant l'occupation anglaise 1417–49* (Lisieux 1936)

Gairdner, J., *Letters and Papers illustrative of the Reigns of Richard III and Henry VII*, I (1861)

Geradon, E. de, *see* 'Corpus des Primitifs Flamands'

Gilliodts-van Severen, L., *Bruges port de mer, étude historique* (1895)
  Cartulaire de l'ancienne estaple de Bruges II (1905): *1451–1544*
  Inventaire des archives de la ville de Bruges: Inventaire des chartes I–VIII (1871–82); *Index*, ed. E. Gailliard, IX–X (1882–5)

Goethe, *Kunst und Altertum* I (1816)

Goethe [and Johann Heinrich Meyer], 'Geschichte des Kolorits seit Wiederherstellung der Kunst', *Farbenlehre* III, v, 24 [1808]

Grunzweig, A., *Correspondance de la filiale de Bruges des Medici* I (1931)

Guicciardini, Lodovico, *Descrittione di tutti i Paesi Bassi* (1567)

Guillaume-Linephty, M., *Hans Memling in the Hospital of St. John at Bruges* (1939)
  La Châsse de Sainte Ursule (1958)

Halliwell, J. O., *see* Warkworth

Harriss, G. L., 'The Struggle for Calais: an aspect of the rivalry between Lancaster and York', *The English Historical Review* LXXV (1960), pp. 30–53

Heinecken, C. H. von, *Nachrichten von Künstlern und Kunstsachen* II (1769)

Heise, C. G., *Der Lübecker Passionsaltar von Hans Memling* (1950)

Henry VIII, Calendar of Letters and Papers, see London, Public Record Office

Hill, G. F., *A Corpus of Italian Medals* (1930)

Hingeston, F. C., *Royal and Historical Letters during the Reign of Henry IV*, I (1860)

Hotho, H. G., *Geschichte der deutschen und niederländischen Malerei* II (1843)

Huizinga, J., *The Waning of the Middle Ages* (1924)

HULIN DE LOO, G., 'Diptychs by Rogier van der Weyden', *The Burlington Magazine* XLIII (1923), pp. 53–7; XLIV (1924) pp. 179–89

'Hans Memling in Rogier van der Weyden's Studio', *The Burlington Magazine* LII (1928), pp. 160–77

'Le portrait du médailleur par Hans Memling: Jean de Candida et non Niccolò Spinelli', in *Festschrift für Max J. Friedländer* (1927), pp. 103–8

HUMBOLDT, Alexander von, *Kosmos* II (1847)

JAMESON, Mrs., *Sacred and Legendary Art* (1848)

KAEMMERER, L., *Memling* (1899)

KEHRER, H., *Die heiligen drei Könige in Literatur und Kunst* (1909)

LABORDE, L. de, *Essai d'un catalogue des artistes originaires des Pays-Bas ou employés à la cour des ducs de Bourgogne aux XIVe et XVe siècles* (1849)

'Inventaire des tableaux, livres, joyaux et meubles de Marguerite d'Autriche . . . fait . . . en la ville d'Anvers le 15 avril 1524', *Revue archéologique* VII (Paris 1850), pp. 36–57; 80–91

Les ducs de Bourgogne II (1851), pp. 293–382: 'Compte des ouvrages et aussi des entremetz et paintures faicts à Bruges, aux nopces de MS le duc Charles, en l'année commençant, en mars, anno LXVII. . . .'

LA MARCHE, Olivier de, *Mémoires*, ed. H. Beaune and J. d'Arbaumont, III (1885)

LARSEN, Erik, *Les primitifs flamands au Musée Métropolitain de New York* (1960)

LAVALLEYE, J., see 'Corpus des primitifs flamands'

LE GLAY, A. J. G., *Correspondance de l'empereur Maximilien Ier et de Marguerite d'Autriche, de 1507 à 1519*, II (1819), pp. 479 ff.: 'Inventoire des painctures fait à Malines'

LIPSCOMB, G., *The History and Antiquities of the County of Buckingham* (1847)

LLOYD, J. E., *Owen Glendower* (1931)

LODGE, E. C., and R. SOMERVILLE, *John of Gaunt's Register, 1379–83* (1937)

London, British Museum Library, *Harleian MS 642*

London, Historical MSS Commission, Report no. 78: *The Manuscripts of R. Rawdon Hastings* (1928–47)

London, Public Record Office, *Annual Reports of the Deputy Keeper* XLIV (1883); XLVIII (1887)

Calendar of Close Rolls 1485–1500 (1955)

Calendar of Fine Rolls 1452–61 (1939)

Calendar of Inquisitions post mortem, Henry VII, I (1898); II (1915); III (1955)

Calendar of Letters and Papers, Foreign and Domestic, of the Reign of Henry VIII, ed. J. S. Brewer, James Gairdner and R. H. Brodie, I (1862, revised 1920); II (1864); III (1867); IV, i (1870); IV, ii (1872); V (1880)

Calendar of Patent Rolls 1413–16 (1910); *1422–9* (1901); *1452–61* (1910); *1461–7* (1897); *1467–77* (1900); *1476–85* (1901); *1485–94* (1914); *1494–1509* (1916)

Descriptive Catalogue of Ancient Deeds III (1900)

MS Exchequer of Receipt, Warrants for Issue, E404/74/1/45

Prerogative Court of Canterbury Wills: 32 Adeane (Elizabeth Donne); *10 Blamyr* (John Donne); *10 Logge* (William Hastings); *F. 1 Powell* (Edward Donne); *7 Pynnyng* (Griffith Donne)

London, Westminster Abbey Muniments 16057

LOVATT, R., 'The "Imitation of Christ" in Late Medieval England', *Transactions of the Royal Historical Society* XVIII (1968), pp. 97–121

Lübeck, Staatsarchiv, *Varia no. 267c*

MCFARLANE, K. B., *The Wars of the Roses* (Raleigh Lecture, British Academy 1964)

MANDER, Karel van, *Het Schilderboeck* (1604)

MATTHEWS, T., *Welsh Records in Paris* (1910)

MESNIL, J., *L'art au nord et au sud des Alpes à l'époque de la Renaissance* (1911)

MEYER, Johann Heinrich, *see* Goethe

MICHEL, Edouard, *Catalogue raisonné des peintures flamandes du XVe et du XVIe siècle, Musée du Louvre* (1953)

[MICHIEL, Marcantonio], *Notizia d'opere di disegno*, ed. Jacopo Morelli (1800)

MYERS, A. R., *The Household of Edward IV* (1959)

NICHOLS, J. Gough, Letter [on the Donne Triptych] in *The Gentleman's Magazine* XIV (1840), pp. 489 ff.

NICOLAS, N. Harris, *Testamenta vetusta* (1826)

   The Controversy between Sir Richard Scrope and Sir Robert Grosvenor in the Court of Chivalry, A.D. 1385–1390 (1832)

Oxford, Bodleian Library, *MS Douce 393*

PÄCHT, O., *The Master of Mary of Burgundy* (1948)

PANOFSKY, E., *Early Netherlandish Painting* (1953)

PAPWORTH, J. W., and A. W. MORANT, *Alphabetical Dictionary of Coats of Arms* (1874)

PARMENTIER, R. A., *Indices op de Brugsche Poorterboeken* (1938)

PERRY, M. P., 'On the Psychostasis in Christian Art', *The Burlington Magazine* XXII (1912–13), pp. 94–105; pp. 208–18

P[HILLIPPS], T[homas], *Cartularium S. Johannis Bapt. de Caermarthen* (1865)

PINCHART, A., 'Roger de la Pasture dit Van der Weyden', *Bulletin des commissions royales d'art et d'archéologie* VI (Brussels 1867), pp. 408 ff.

POWER, E., and M. M. POSTAN, *Studies in English Trade in the Fifteenth Century* (1933)

PRIMS, F., 'Het schip van Portunari, 1473–1498', *Antwerpiensia* XII (1939), nos. 12 f., pp. 76–89

PUYVELDE, L. van, *La peinture flamande au siècle des Van Eyck* (1953)

RACKHAM, B., *Catalogue of Italian Maiolica, Victoria and Albert Museum* (1940)

   Italian Maiolica (1952)

RAMSAY, J. H., *Lancaster and York, 1399–1485* (1892)

REUMONT, A., 'Di alcune relazioni dei Fiorentini colla città di Danzica', *Archivio storico italiano* XIII (1861), pp. 37–47

RODENBACH, G., *Bruges-la-Morte* (1892)

ROOVER, R. de, *Money, Banking and Credit in Mediaeval Bruges* (1948)

ROPP, G. von der, *Hanserecesse von 1431–1476*, VII (1892)

'Zur Geschichte des Alaunhandels im fünfzehnten Jahrhundert', *Hansische Geschichtsblätter* (1901), pp. 117–36

ROSSETTI, Dante Gabriel, *Sonnets* [on Memling], in *The Germ* (1850)

Rotuli Parliamentorum IV [1770]: *1413–37*

RUMOHR, C. F. von, 'Einige Nachrichten von Altertümern des transalbingischen Sachsens', *Deutsches Museum*, ed. F. Schlegel, IV (1813), pp. 479–516

[RUMOHR, C. F. von], *Altargemälde der Greveraden-Kapelle im Dom zu Lübeck*, reproduced in lithograph by Carl Julius Milde, Erwin and Otto Speckter (1825)

RYMER, T., *Fœdera* XI (1710): *1441–75*; XII (1711): *1475–1502*; XIII (1712): *1502–23*

SALTER, H. E., *The Boarstall Cartulary* (1930)

SCHESTAG, A., 'Die Chronik von Jerusalem', *Jahrbuch der kunsthistorischen Sammlungen des Allerhöchsten Kaiserhauses in Wien* XX (1899), pp. 195–216

SCHINKEL, C. F., *Aus Schinkels Nachlass*, ed. A. von Wolzogen, II (1862)

Aus Tagebüchern und Briefen, ed. Günter Meier (1967)

SCHLEGEL, Friedrich, *Deutsches Museum* (1812–13)

Gemäldebeschreibungen aus Paris und den Niederlanden in den Jahren 1802–1804, reprinted in *Sämtliche Werke* VI (1846), pp. 7–170

SCHNAASE, Carl, *Geschichte der bildenden Künste* VIII (1879)

SCHÖNE, W., *Dieric Bouts und seine Schule* (1938)

'Hans Memling: zur Ausstellung seines Lebenswerkes in Brügge', *Pantheon* XXIV (1939), pp. 291–9

SCHOPENHAUER, Johanna, *Johannes van Eyck und seine Nachfolger* (1822)

SCOFIELD, C. L., *The Life and Reign of Edward IV* (1923)

SHAW, W. A., *The Knights of England* (1906)

SITWELL, Dom Gerard, *Medieval Spiritual Writers* (1961)

SOSSON, J.-P., *Les primitifs flamands de Bruges: apports des archives contemporaines, 1815–1907* (1966)

[STENDHAL], *Lettres écrites de Vienne en Autriche sur le célèbre compositeur Jh Haydn, suivies d'une vie de Mozart et de considérations sur Métastase et l'état présent de la musique en France et en Italie* (1814), with reflection on the Danzig *Last Judgement* in the Musée Napoléon (Letter, 1809)

STEVENSON, J., *Letters and Papers illustrative of the Wars of the English in France during the Reign of Henry VI, King of England* (1861).

VAN MOLLE, Frans, *Identification d'un portrait de Gilles Joye attribué à Memlinc* (1960)

VANDEN HAUTE, Charles, *La Corporation des Peintres de Bruges* (Bruges n.d.)

VARCHI, Benedetto, *Storia fiorentina*, ed. G. Milanesi (1857)

VASARI, Giorgio, *Vite de' più eccellenti pittori, scultori e architetti*, ed. G. Milanesi (1878–1885)

VOLL, K., *Memling* (1909)

WAAGEN, G. F., *Über Hubert und Jan van Eyck* (1822)
   Works of Art and Artists in England (1838)

WARBURG, A., *Flandrische Kunst und florentinische Frührenaissance* (1902); reprinted in
   Gesammelte Schriften (1932), pp. 182–206, 370–80

WARKWORTH, John, *A Chronicle of the First Thirteen Years of the Reign of King Edward
   IV*, ed. J. O. Halliwell (1839)

WAURIN, Jehan de, *Recueil des croniques et anchiennes istories de la Grant Bretaigne* IV,
   1431–1447, ed. W. Hardy and E. L. C. P. Hardy (1884)

WAUTERS, A. J. 'Memling', *Biographie nationale de Belgique* XIV (1890), pp. 340–57
   Sept études pour servir à l'histoire de Hans Memling (Brussels 1893)

WEALE, W. H. J., *Bruges et ses environs* (1862)
   Catalogue du Musée de l'Académie de Bruges (1861)
   'Documents authentiques concernant la vie, la famille et la position sociale de Jean
      Memlinc', *Journal des beaux-arts et de la littérature* (Brussels 1861), pp. 21–55, 196
   'Documents inédits sur les enlumineurs de Bruges', *Le Beffroi* IV (1872–3), pp. 111–19,
      238–337
   'Généalogie de la famille Moreel', *Le Beffroi* II (1865), pp. 179–96
   Hans Memlinc (1901)
   'Inventaire du mobilier de la Corporation des Tanneurs de Bruges', *Le Beffroi* II (1865),
      pp. 264–74
   'L'école de Bruges et les Annales Archéologiques de Paris', *Le Beffroi* I (1863), pp. 65–
      71
   'Memling's Passion Picture in the Turin Gallery', *The Burlington Magazine* XII (1908),
      pp. 309 ff.
   'Triptych by Hans Memling at Chiswick', *Notes and Queries* VI (1864), pp. 451 f.
   'Voll's *Memling*', review in *The Burlington Magazine* XV (1909), pp. 313 ff.

WEDGWOOD, J. C., *History of Parliament: Biographies of the members of the Commons
   house, 1439–1509* (1936)

WEHLE, H. B., and M. SALINGER, *Catalogue of Early Flemish, Dutch and German
   Paintings, The Metropolitan Museum of Art* (1947)

WINKLER, F., *Die altniederländische Malerei* (1924)
   Die flämische Buchmalerei des XV. und XVI. Jahrhunderts (1925)

WORCESTRE, William, *Itineraries*, ed. John H. Harvey (1969)

WURZBACH, A. von, 'Vrelant', in *Niederländisches Künstlerlexikon* II (1910), pp. 826 ff.

XELLER, Christian, 'Über das Jüngste Gericht in der Pfarrkirche in Danzig', *Neue
   Preussische Provinzialblätter* I (1852), pp. 71–80

Index

Anchorites, *see* hermit-saints

Anglo, S., 54 n.

Anonimo Morelliano, see Michiel, Marcantonio

Anthony of Burgundy, 36, fig. 139

Antwerp inventory of paintings belonging to Margaret of Austria, 36 n.

Antwerp, Musée des Beaux-Arts: Memling, *Portrait of a Man holding a coin of Nero*, 14 f., 42, fig. 141

Apocalyptic vision (Memling), 39 n., fig. 32

'Apotheosis of the Van Eycks' proposed by Schinkel, 37 n.

Archaisms in Roger van der Weyden, 39, 43 f.

Armagnac, Général d', 31 n.

ars nova, 42

Aru, C., 32 n.

Augustine, on the imperishable flesh of the peacock, 18 n.

Auqueville, lordship conferred on Griffith Donne, 6 n.

Baldass, L. von, 21, 36 n.

Baroncelli, Maria, wife of Tommaso Portinari, 13, 32 n., 33 n., 34 n., 41 n., figs. 76, 134, 136

Basle, Öffentliche Kunstsammlung: Memling (copy), *Portrait of James of Savoy*, 36 n.

Beaune, Hôtel Dieu: Roger van der Weyden, *The Annunciation* (grisaille), 39, fig. 110; *The Last Judgement*, 18 ff., 24 f., 40 n., figs. 44, 49, 50

Beenken, H., 39 n.

Bembo, Pietro, 30 n., 35

Berlin-Dahlem, Staatliche Museen: Memling Workshop, *Virgin and Child*, 38 n., 42 n., fig. 146; Petrus Christus, *The Last Judgement*, 22; Roger van der Weyden, *Martyrdom of St. John the Baptist*, from the St. John's Triptych, 13, fig. 28

Bernardino da Siena, badge of, 42 n., figs. 145, 146

Bernewall, Robert, 7 n.

Bialostocki, J., 19 n., 24

Bisthoven, A. Janssens de, 31 n.

Boarstall, Bucks, 8 n., 53

Bock, Franz, 5 n.

Boisserée, Mathilde, 31 n.

Boisserée, Melchior, 36 n.

Boisserée, Sulpiz, 31 n., 36 n., 38 n., 40

Boisserée Collection, bought by Ludwig I of Bavaria, 31 n.; place of Memling in it, 38 n.

Boteler, Sir John, 54 n.

Boulogne, siege of (1492), 10 n.

Bouts, Dieric, 16, 22 f., figs. 59, 60

Brandon, Charles, 54

Bray, Sir Reynold, 3 n.

Brewer, J. S., 8 n., 10 n., 54 n.

Brockwell, M.W., 24, 29 n.

Brömbsen, Lübeck family, 35 n.

Brouning, William sr., effigy in Melbury Sampford Church, Dorset, 4 n.

Browne, Sir Anthony, 10 n.

Bruce, J., 53

Bruges, archives, 10 n., 16 n., 17 n., 28 n.; banking houses, 25 f., 26 n., 28, 34 f., 35 n.; cloth industry, 28; guilds, 30, 31, 32, 33 n.; harbour, 17 n., 28 n.; relations with the Hanse, 16 n., 17 n.; restitution of works of art from Paris (1816), 36 n.; wedding celebrations for Charles of Burgundy and Margaret of York, 3 f., 10, 26 n., 30

Bruges, churches: St. Donation, 28 n., 43 n.; St. Giles, 28 n.; St. James, 31

Bruges, Hospital of St. John, 10, 11, 33 f.; works by Memling: *Jan Floreins Altarpiece*, 12, 33, figs. 11, 13, 14; *Martin van Nieuwenhove Diptych*, 13, 25, 31, 35 n. 41, figs. 151–2; *Adriaen Reyns Altarpiece*, 10 n., 33, figs. 15–23; *St. John's Altarpiece*, 4, 10 f., 12, 13, 21 n., 31 n., 33 f., 39 n., 55, figs. 24–7, 29–36; *The Shrine of St. Ursula*, 28 n., 31 n., 34, figs. 98–108

Bruges, museums:

Musée Communal des Beaux-Arts: Memling, *Moreel Altarpiece*, 2 n., 31, 36 n., 41, figs. 82–91

Musée Saint-Sauveur: *Le Calvaire des Tanneurs* (fourteenth-century *Crucifixion* formerly in the chapel of the Tanners' Guild), 45 n.

Brussels, Musée Royal des Beaux-Arts: Memling, *Martyrdom of St. Sebastian*, 45 n., fig. 131; *Portraits of Willem and Barbara Moreel*, 31, figs. 92–3; *Portrait of a Man*, 14, fig. 148

Bultync, Adriaen, son of Pieter and Katelyne Bultync, 30, fig. 80

Bultync, Josse, father of Pieter Bultync, 30 n.

Bultync, Katelyne, 30 n., fig. 81

Bultync, Pieter, 12, 30, 40, 41 n., fig. 80

Burckhardt, Jacob, 34 n.

Burgundian court, *see* Anthony of Burgundy; Charles the Bold; Mary of Burgundy; Philip the Good; for Margaret of Burgundy *see* Margaret of York

Burne-Jones, Edward, 37 n.

Caermarthen, 6 n.

Calais, 7 n., 9 f., 10 n., 54 n., 55

Calendars of Close Rolls, 10 n.; Fine Rolls, 2 n.; Inquisitions post mortem, 8 n., 9 n.; Patent Rolls, 4 n., 6 n., 7 n., 9 n., 55 n.

Calkewell, John Bunolt of, 10 n.

Camoys, Alice, 7

Candida, Giovanni, 14

Canigiani, Gherardo, 26 n.

PLATES

1. Memling: The Donne Altarpiece, central panel. National Gallery, London

2. Memling: St. Catherine. Detail from fig. 1

3. Memling: Portrait of Sir John Donne. Detail from fig. 1

4. Memling: Portrait of Lady Donne, with her daughter Anne. Detail from fig. 1

5. Memling: St. Barbara. Detail from fig. 1

6. Memling: Coat of arms of the Donnes of Kidwelly. Detail from fig. 1

7. Memling: Coat of arms of Hastings impaled with Donne. Detail from fig. 1

8. Memling: The Donne Triptych opened. National Gallery, London

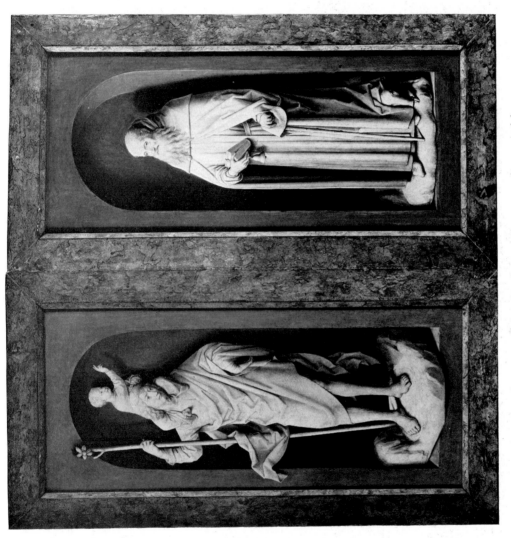

9. Memling: St. Christopher and St. Anthony Abbot.
Shutters of the Donne Triptych. National Gallery, London

10. Memling: St. John the Baptist, with onlooker. Detail from fig. 8

11. Memling: Detail from the Jan Floreins Altarpiece (fig. 14): Joseph, Magus and onlooker

12. Memling: Details of onlookers, from Adorations of the Magi.
Museo del Prado, Madrid; Alte Pinakothek, Munich

13. Memling: Portrait of Jan Floreins, aged 36, with attendant. Detail from fig. 14

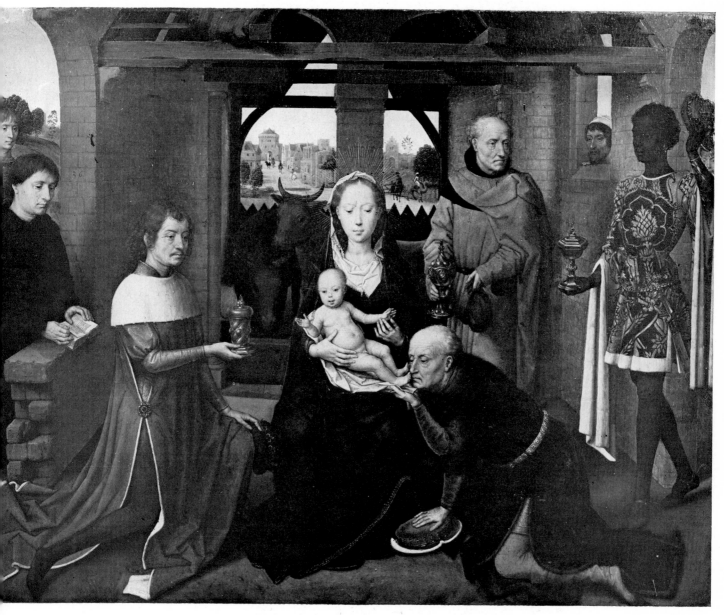

4. Memling: The Adoration Of The Magi, central panel of the Jan Floreins Altarpiece. St. John's Hospital, Bruges

15. Memling: St. Adrian, with Adriaen Reyns as donor. Detail from fig. 17

16. Memling: St. Wilgefortis and St. Mary of Egypt.
Shutters of the Reyns Triptych (fig. 17)

17. Memling: The Reyns Triptych opened. St. John's Hospital, Bruges

18. Memling: St. Adrian, holding the anvil. Detail from fig. 17

19. Memling: St. Barbara. Detail from fig. 17

20. Memling: Portrait of Adriaen Reyns. Detail from fig. 17

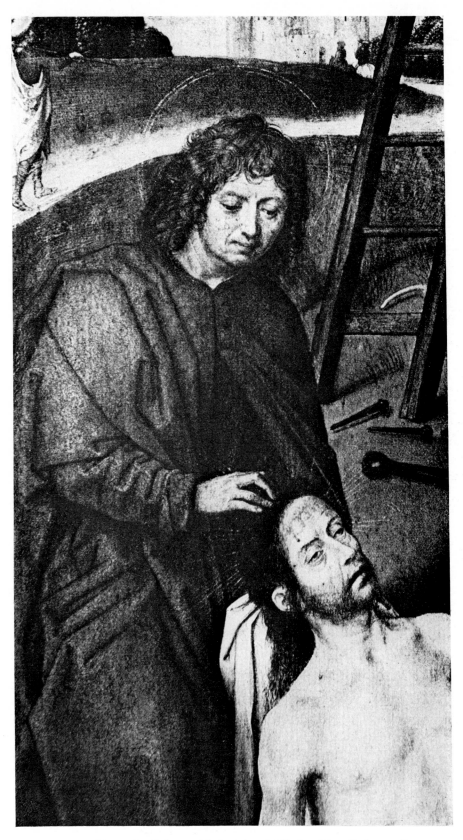

21. Memling: St. John and the dead Christ. Detail from fig. 17

22. Memling: St. Wilgefortis, bearded. Detail from fig. 16

23. Memling: St. Mary of Egypt. Detail from fig. 16

24. Memling: Portraits of Antonis Seghers and Jacob de Kueninc,
with their patron saints St. Anthony Abbot and St. James.
Shutters of the St. John's Altarpiece (fig. 35)

25. Memling: Portraits of Agnes Casembrood and Clara van Hulsen,
with their patron saints St. Agnes and St. Clare.
Shutters of the St. John's Altarpiece (fig. 35)

26. Memling: Martyrdom of St. John the Baptist.
Left wing of the St. John's Altarpiece (fig. 35)

27. Memling: St. John baptizing Christ in the Jordan. Detail from the background of fig. 26

28. Roger van der Weyden: Martyrdom of St. John the Baptist. Staatliche Museen, Berlin-Dahlem

29. Memling: Salome receiving the head of St. John the Baptist. Detail from fig. 26

30. Memling: The Virgin. Detail from fig. 14

31. Memling: Salome. Detail from fig. 26

32. Memling: Apocalyptic Vision. Detail from fig. 33

33. Memling: St. John on Patmos.
Right wing of the St. John's Altarpiece (fig. 35),
St. John's Hospital, Bruges

34. Memling: St. John the Evangelist, with onlooker. Detail from fig. 35

35. Memling: Holy Conversation — 'The Mystic Marriage of St. Catherine',
central panel of the St. John's Triptych. St. John's Hospital, Bruges

36. Memling: Virgin and Child. Detail from fig. 35

37. Memling: Virgin and Child. Detail from the Donne Triptych (fig. 1)

38. Memling: Virgin and Child, with donor and St. Anthony Abbot. National Gallery of Canada, Ottawa

39. Memling: The Annunciation. Collection Robert Lehman, New York

40. 'Memling': St. Michael weighing the Souls.
Detail from the central panel of the Danzig Last Judgement (fig. 45, 51)

41. 'Memling': Angelo Tani and his wife Catarina protected by St. Michael and the Virgin.
Shutters of the Danzig Last Judgement (figs. 45, 51)

42. 'Memling': Portrait of Angelo Tani. Detail from fig. 41

43. 'Memling': Portrait of Catarina Tani. Detail from fig. 41

44. Roger van der Weyden: Central panel of the Beaune Last Judgement (fig. 50)

45. 'Memling': Central panel of the Danzig Last Judgement (fig. 51)

46. 'Memling': Rising of the Dead, mirrored in the armour of St. Michael. Detail from fig. 40

47. 'Memling': Heavenly Host and St. Michael mirrored in the globe under Christ's feet. Detail from fig. 48

48. 'Memling': Christ as Judge, seated on rainbow. Detail from fig. 51

49. Roger van der Weyden: Christ as Judge, seated on rainbow. Detail from fig. 50

50. Roger van der Weyden: The Last Judgement. Hotel Dieu, Beaune

51. 'Memling': The Last Judgement. Marienkirche, Danzig

52. 'Memling': Pious Souls at the Resurrection. Detail from fig. 45

53. 'Memling': Souls rising from their tombs. Detail from fig. 52

54. 'Memling': Souls saved. Detail from fig. 51

55. 'Memling': Souls damned. Detail from fig. 51

56. 'Memling': Souls in Hell. Detail from fig. 51

57. 'Memling': A Devil. Detail from figs. 51, 58

58. 'Memling': Souls in Hell. Detail from fig. 51

59. Dieric Bouts: Souls in Hell. Louvre, Paris

60. Dieric Bouts: The Fountain of Life (companion piece to fig. 59). Musée des Beaux-Arts, Lille

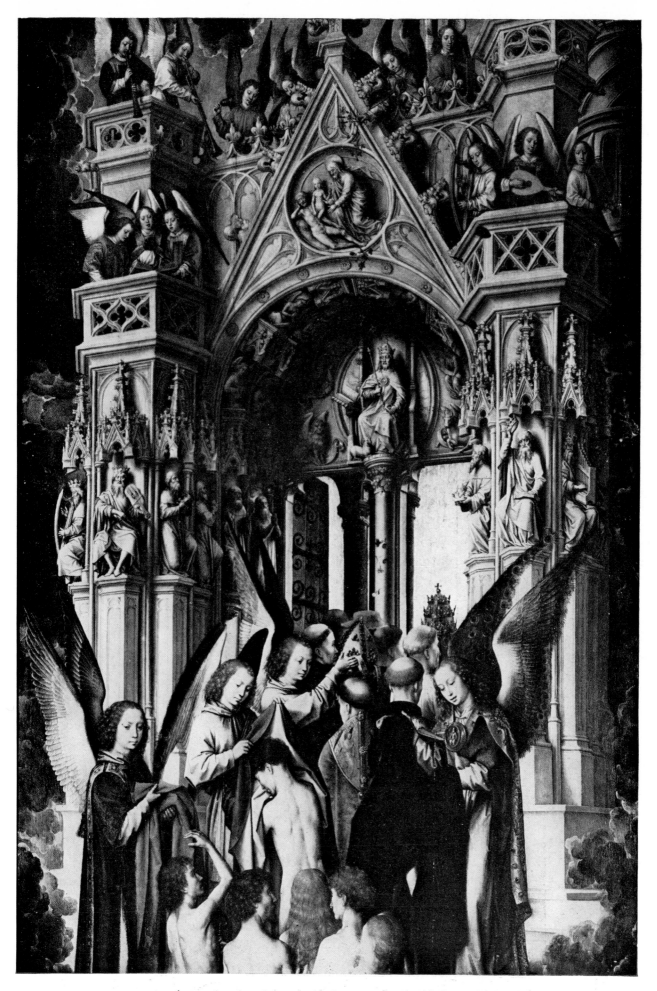

61. 'Memling': The Gates of Heaven. Detail from fig. 62

62. 'Memling': Souls received at the Gates of Heaven. Left wing of the Danzig Last Judgement (fig. 51)

63. 'Memling': St. Peter receiving the Blessed. Detail from fig. 62. Infra-red photograph

64. 'Memling': Saved Souls. Detail from fig. 62

65. 'Memling': Saved Soul approaching the Gates of Heaven. Detail from fig. 62

66. 'Memling': Saved Soul and Angel. Detail from fig. 62

67. 'Memling': Detail from the Weighing of Souls, fig. 45.
Infra-red photograph (the head painted in 1851)

68. 'Memling': Resurrected Soul sitting on tomb-slab,
with inscription ANNO DOMINI [MC]CCCLXVII. Detail from fig. 52

69. Memling: Adam and Eve. Kunsthistorisches Museum, Vienna

70. Memling: Panorama of the Passion. Galleria Sabauda, Turin

71. Memling: Panorama of Epiphanies ('The Star of Bethlehem'). Alte Pinakothek, Munich

72. Memling: Ecce Homo. Detail from fig. 70

73. Memling: The Last Supper, with The Departure of Judas (on the left). Detail from fig. 70

74. Memling: Golgotha. Detail from fig. 70

75. Memling: Presumed portrait of Tommaso Portinari as donor of
the Panorama of the Passion. Detail from fig. 70

76. Memling: Presumed portrait of Maria Portinari.
Detail from fig. 70

77. Memling: Magi on the mountains, watching the Star of Bethlehem. Detail from fig. 71

78. Memling: Procession of the Magi. Detail from fig. 71

79. Memling: Page with Horses. Detail from fig. 71

80. Memling: Pieter Bultync and his son Adriaen, attending the Nativity. Detail from fig. 71

81. Memling: Katelyne Bultync, attending the Pentecost. Detail from fig. 71

82. Memling: Willem Moreel with his Sons, protected by St. William of Maleval.
Left wing of the Moreel Triptych. Musée Communal des Beaux-Arts, Bruges

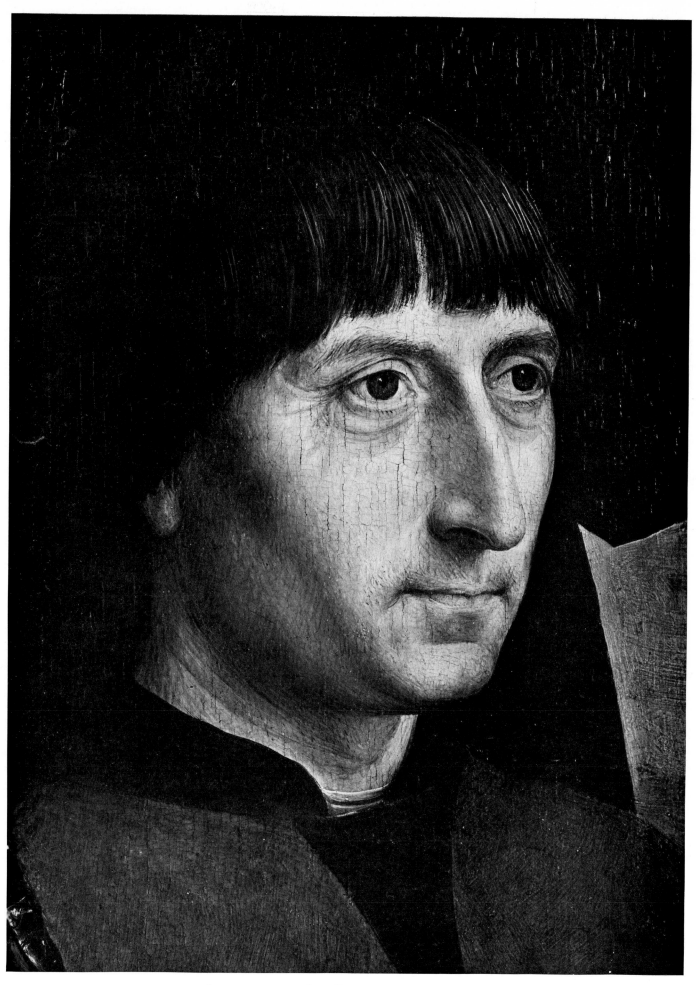

83. Memling: Portrait of Willem Moreel. Detail from fig. 82

84. Memling: Portrait of Barbara Moreel. Detail from fig. 85

85. Memling: Barbara Moreel with her Daughters, protected by St. Barbara.
Right wing of the Moreel Triptych. Musée Communal des Beaux-Arts, Bruges

86. Memling: The Hermit's Lamp. Detail from fig. 87

87. Memling: St. Christopher between St. Maur and St. Giles.
Central panel of the Moreel Triptych. Musée Communal des Beaux-Arts, Bruges

88. Memling: St. Maur. Detail from fig. 87

89. Memling: St. Giles. Detail from fig. 87

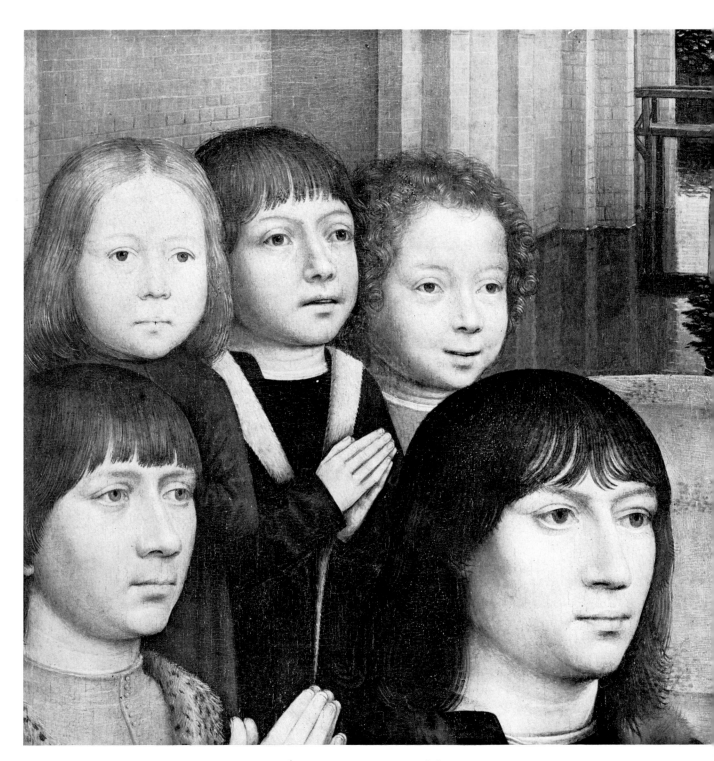

90. Memling: Five Sons. Detail from fig. 82

91. Memling: Eleven Daughters. Detail from fig. 85

92. Memling: Portrait of Willem Moreel. Musée Royal des Beaux-Arts, Brussels

93. Memling: Portrait of Barbara Moreel. Musée Royal des Beaux-Arts, Brussels

94. Memling: Portrait of Jacob Floreins. Detail from fig. 95

95. Memling: Jacob Floreins Altarpiece. Louvre, Paris

96. Memling: Seven Sons of Jacob Floreins.
Detail from fig. 95

97. Memling: Twelve Daughters. Detail from fig. 95

98. Memling: St. Ursula with her Companions. Detail from the Shrine of St. Ursula (fig. 99)

99. Shrine of St. Ursula. St. John's Hospital, Bruges

100. Memling: Coronation of the Virgin. Detail from fig. 99

101. Memling: St. Ursula with her Companions. Detail from fig. 102

102. Shrine of St. Ursula. St. John's Hospital, Bruges

103. Memling: The Virgin and Child, with the donors of the Shrine of St. Ursula,
presumably Josina van Dudzeele and Anna van den Moortele

104. Memling: St. Ursula arriving at Cologne. Detail from fig. 102

105. Memling: The Vision of St. Ursula. Detail from fig. 104

106. Memling: St. Ursula's Embarkment at Basle, with Pope, Cardinals and Bishop. Detail from fig. 99

107. Memling: Martyrdom in Cologne. Detail from fig. 99

108. Memling: Angel singing to the lute. Detail from fig. 99

109. Memling: Angel with sword (fragment).
Wallace Collection, London

110. Roger van der Weyden: The Annunciation.
Grisaille from the shutters of the Beaune Altarpiece (fig. 50)

111. Memling: The Annunciation.
Grisaille from the shutters of the Lübeck Altarpiece (fig. 121)

112–115. Memling: St. Blaise, St. John the Baptist, St. Jerome, St. Giles.

Inner shutters of the Lübeck Altarpiece (fig. 121)

116. Memling: The Good Thief on the Cross. Detail from fig. 121

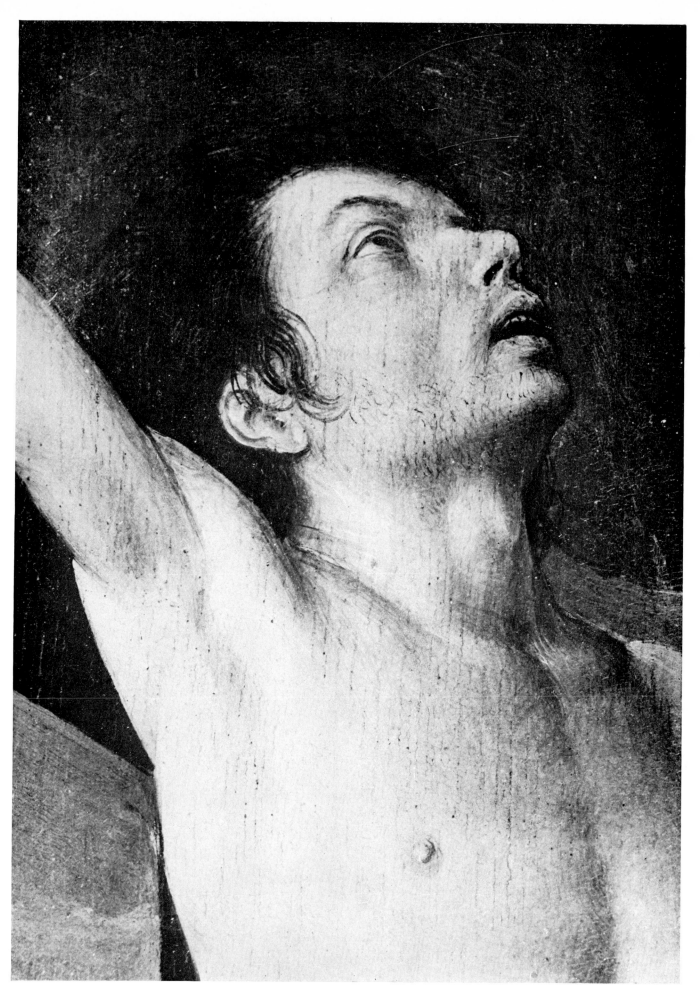

117. Memling: The Good Thief. Detail from fig. 121

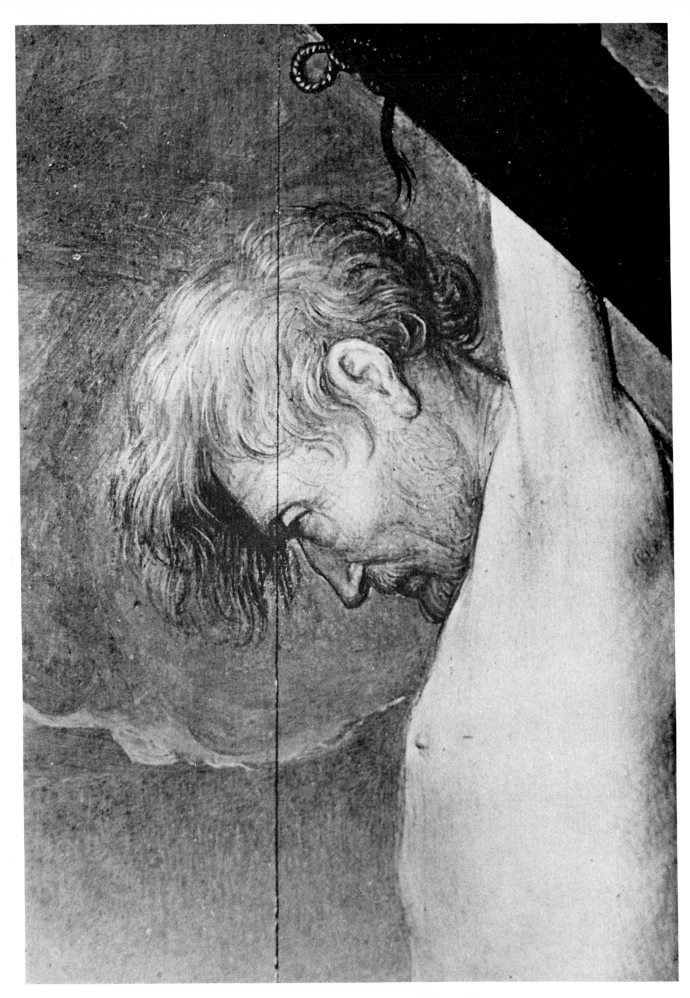

118. Memling: The Evil Thief. Detail from fig. 119

119. Memling: The Evil Thief on the Cross. Detail from fig. 121

120. Memling: Portrait of Heinrich Greverade, donor of the Lübeck Altarpiece.
Detail from the left wing of fig. 121

121. Memling: Triptych of the Passion. Domkirche, Lübeck

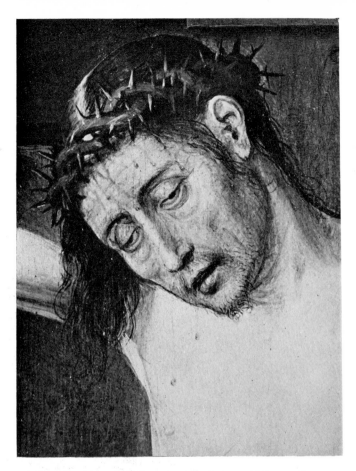

122. Memling: Christ crucified. Detail from fig. 121

123. Memling: Soldiers below the Cross. Detail from fig. 121

124. Memling: A Pharisee and two Levites (?) attending the Crucifixion. Detail from fig. 121

125. Memling: The Virgin under the Cross. Detail from fig. 121

126. Memling: Christ resurrected. Detail from fig. 121

127. Memling: *Noli me tangere*. Detail from fig. 121

128. Memling: The Road to Emmaus. Detail from fig. 121

129. Memling: The Ascension. Detail from fig. 121

130. Memling: Peter trying to walk on the water. Detail from fig. 121

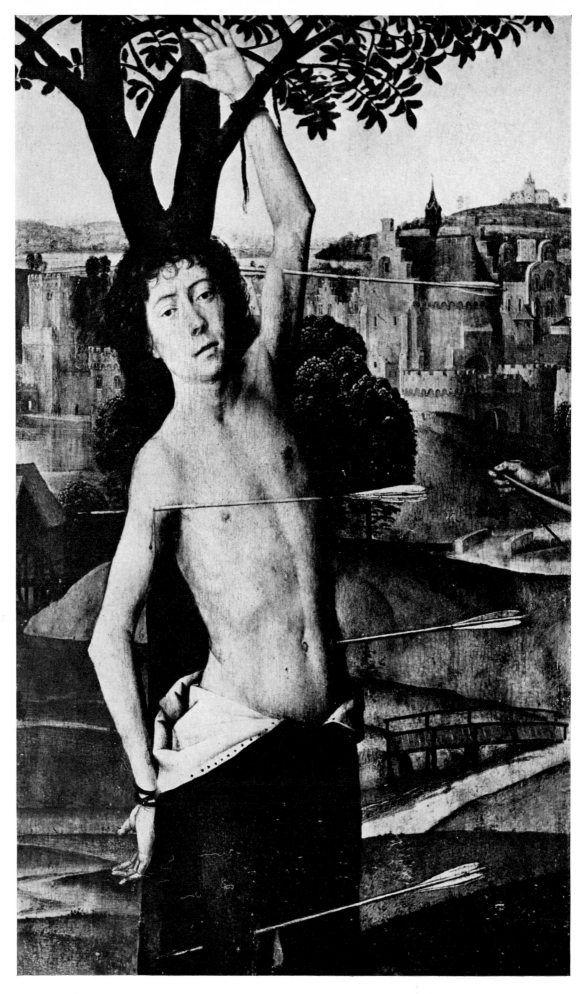

131. Memling: Martyrdom of St. Sebastian (detail). Musée Royal des Beaux-Arts, Brussels

132. Memling: Veronica's Napkin (detail). National Gallery of Art, Washington

133. Memling: Portrait of Tommaso Portinari. Metropolitan Museum of Art, New York

134. Memling: Portrait of Maria Portinari. Metropolitan Museum of Art, New York

135. Hugo van der Goes: Portrait of Tommaso Portinari.
From the Triptych of the Nativity, Uffizi, Florence

136. Hugo van der Goes: Portrait of Maria Portinari.
From the Triptych of the Nativity, Uffizi, Florence

137. Memling: Lady with a Pink.
Metropolitan Museum of Art, New York

138. Memling: Horses with Monkey,
emblematic design.
Museum Boymans-van Beunigen, Rotterdam

139. Memling (copy): Portrait of Antoine de Bourgogne.
Musée Condé, Chantilly

140. Memling: Portrait of an Italian (?). Uffizi, Florence

141. Memling: Portrait of a Man holding a coin of Nero. Musée des Beaux-Arts, Antwerp

142a. Memling: Landscape with palm tree. Detail from fig. 141

142b. Sestertius of Nero.
Ashmolean Museum, Oxford

143. Memling: Portrait of a Youth. National Gallery, London

144. Memling: Portrait of a Young Man in Prayer. Obverse of fig. 145. Collection Thyssen-Bornemisza, Lugano

145. Memling: Flowers sacred to the Virgin.
Reverse of fig. 144. Collection Thyssen-Bornemisza, Lugano

146. Memling Workshop: Virgin and Child (detail). Staatliche Museen, Berlin-Dahlem

147. Memling: Portrait of a Man. Mauritshuis, The Hague

148. Memling: Portrait of a Man. Musée Royal des Beaux-Arts, Brussels

149. Memling: St. Benedict. Companion piece of fig. 150. Uffizi, Florence

150. Memling: Portrait of Benedetto Portinari. Companion piece of fig. 149. Uffizi, Florence

151. Memling: Virgin and Child, left wing of the Nieuwenhove Diptych.
St. John's Hospital, Bruges

152. Memling: Portrait of Martin van Nieuwenhove adoring the Virgin and Child (fig. 151).
St. John's Hospital, Bruges

153. Memling: Window with coat of arms of the Donnes of Kidwelly. Detail from fig. 8